Counselling
Drug Abus

CW00364030

By the same author

MICROSCOPE ON BONDAGE

Frank Wilson

Counselling the Drug Abuser

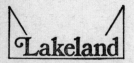

LAKELAND
116 Baker Street
LONDON WIM 2BB.

Copyright © Frank Wilson, 1973

First published 1973

ISBN 0 551 00478 9

Printed in Great Britain by
Cox & Wyman Ltd,
London, Reading and Fakenham

CONTENTS

Preface

In 1964 my wife and I began a mission to the many young drug addicts of London, working in the name of Jesus Christ. As an outcome of our work, in 1967 a charitable trust was established to help these young people, called 'Life for the World'.

When I went to London, as a very young minister within the Baptist denomination, I knew nothing about the drug problem in England, except that it was fast becoming a real concern to many. I was given the opportunity of working as an unofficial chaplain under the direction of Dr Peter Chapple in the drug unit at West Park Hospital, Surrey, where I spent almost two years alongside the doctors and therapists, working, watching and learning, usually silently. After those two years I was convinced that there came a moment in the cure of the addict when the doctor's help became not only superfluous but positively unhelpful to the patient. Certainly the doctor needs to care for the addict through the pre-withdrawal period, and to carry out the treatment. The many physiological side-effects of drug abuse call for the doctor's skill and healing. Much of the psychological dependence upon drugs also requires the psychiatrist's knowledge and therapeutic help during and immediately after withdrawal. However, there comes a moment when the patient needs to be taken out of the medical and psychiatric environment and given a fresh start in completely new surroundings.

There are many ways and places in which the

addict can be helped in this next step. Although methods may vary and responses will vary, too, from patient to patient, it is necessary for him to be removed from a drug-orientated environment, be it hospital, treatment clinic, community project in which drugs are prescribed, or just general social climate. I appreciate that not everyone will respond to my approach, but I am experienced only in this particular one.

Eighty miles from London we have a country house and farm which we have been using since 1967 as a spiritual therapeutic centre for the rehabilitation of drug addicts. Since the centre opened, more than 150 addict residents have lived with us there. Most have been addicted to heroin and the like, but in recent years increasing numbers of our residents have also used other substances, such as amphetamines and barbiturates. In addition we have, from time to time, taken in those who have been seriously affected by the continued use of cannabis and, on a lesser scale, those whose minds have become damaged by the use of LSD. Of all the residents, well over 60 per cent have completed the course of six to twelve months' rehabilitation. Of that number between 55 and 60 per cent have stayed off drugs and have taken up responsible places in society.

Something like 100 people are referred to us annually and all of these are followed through by our own staff and voluntary workers. Sometimes a probation officer or social worker will contact our London centre, a house in the East End with accommodation for house-parents, one other staff member and eight residents. We take an addict into

8

this half-way house for a maximum period of one week in order to assess his real need, and to decide whether it would be beneficial for him to come into our rehabilitation centre. He may be on remand from the courts or in the final stages of withdrawal. (We have a number of volunteer nurses who assist at this stage when necessary and a doctor who cares for those who come into the London centre.)

Others, who are referred directly to the rehabilitation centre, attend there for interview. During the visit and the interview with a senior staff member or myself, the prospective resident is able to see that a spiritually orientated community can and does work. He will find that people who once had the same drug problem as himself talk freely about God and Jesus Christ. And they not only talk about their faith, they show it by their genuine love and caring for one another and their desire to see the newcomer healed and finding a whole new direction in his life. In the interview he is encouraged to see that it is not enough to 'give up' his drugs—he must adopt a whole new way of life. Religious conversion produces this change, for in the Scriptures we see the highest standards laid down for the person who professes belief in God, and also the offer of a power or dynamic to carry him through. By the time a young man has been in our centre for a few weeks, he ceases to talk about his drug 'hang-ups', but concentrates instead on the reasons why he turned to drugs in the first place. These reasons, of course, are many and varied, but making a deep commitment to Jesus Christ helps a man to come to terms with what his real problems are.

There are a good many rules at Northwick Park and these are self-enforced, out of a sense of responsibility and concern for the rest of the community and for God. If a resident should break a rule, he talks quietly to a staff member about the real problem at the root of the rebellion. Often in our chapel meetings, the person who has broken a rule and offended the rest will humbly ask forgiveness of the community and this is freely and gladly given.

Gradually a young man is able to discover himself in an atmosphere of real love. When a man enters into a relationship with Jesus Christ, Christ meets him at his point of need, his heart, his unconscious self. Call it what you will, but there is indeed an inner man which exists beyond the reach of the most skilful therapist. In the life-changing experience of conversion to Christ feelings of rebellion, bitterness and inadequacy are taken away and the one-time drug-user becomes free in an entirely new way.

The residents at Northwick Park stay from six to twelve months. During what might be called a 're-entry' period, we encourage them to look for jobs and new homes (if their parents can't cope or are too old), away from their old haunts. Here local churches and groups of spiritually minded people can help immensely and often do. In a church group there is a ready-made therapeutic community, perhaps somewhat untrained, but there all the same. We are able to link many of our residents to good homes and youth groups which are willing to take a responsibility for their long-term after-care.

The boys have to work a full eight hours a day, except when there are group meetings. They are divided into different work groups under separate management. Evening activities are varied, from simple relaxation round the television set to chapel services, from Bible studies to more cultural pursuits such as music appreciation, art or cookery. The latter classes are taken by my wife, and it is quite a sight to see the boys in a cloud of flour or with hands deep in dough!

We have a fully trained psychiatric nurse on the staff, and a general nurse. They work as spiritual counsellors much of the time and the professional duties they carry out are very often domestic matters. All of our staff come to work here out of a sense of 'call' and see their responsibility as being ultimately to God. They receive an absolute minimum salary and work on an almost twenty-four hour basis. Their high sense of responsibility and love for their work are part of the reason why we see so much encouragement. The residents sense that the staff are helping them not out of duty, but out of a genuine love for them created by their own love for God.

Group meetings three times a week take the form of discussion and teaching on many subjects related to the new life to which we are introducing residents. Sometimes a visiting speaker will present a series of lectures on related biblical subjects. It surprises many people how eager these young men are to learn from the Scriptures how to live without drugs and in a right relationship with their fellow man. It is in these 'Growth Groups' as they are called that we are able, by love, teaching and precept, to steer the former addict away from his previous cultural thought patterns, to encourage him to think them through and reject all that is negative, so that he can adopt new thoughts and ideas based on an 'absolute standard' of truth as it is in God's Word. Perhaps the most often repeated lesson is the lesson of love. Gradually, in this kind of environment and with the teaching in the Growth Groups, the resident begins to adopt a whole new outlook on life, based on the authority of the Bible.

In the Growth Group we teach, among other things, that the child of God must honour law and the authorities. Slowly these lads learn that the law and its custodians are not bad as they have convinced themselves, but usually good, kind and willing to help in many ways. We also spend time in the Growth Groups and in other group activities dealing with attitudes of resentment and bitterness towards other members of the community, parents and society in general. In contrast to the 'encounter' groups held by some establishments, these groups are conducted around the Bible and in an atmosphere of forbearance, tolerance and love. Obviously such a policy is open to abuse and, from time to time, residents who for one reason or another feel rebellious react against the love of the staff and other residents.

So, there is a brief sketch of our way of helping drug addicts. In this book I will be exploring in more detail different aspects of the problem of drug addiction and the ways in which Christians can help.

Some people may feel that our way is too

simple, 'unprofessional'. However, it is our way, or rather God's way. It works for many. We believe that we are meeting the drug addict at his point of greatest need—his heart, his spiritual being; and let's face it, most people have a need there—a need, often unexpressed or unformulated, for love, for a meaning in life and, in an increasingly insecure world, for the security of knowing that you belong and are related to a power bigger than yourself.

1 / Involvement

To many professional people who work in the context of complex social problems such as that of drug addiction, the idea of involvement is highly suspect. If you were to ask most trained social workers what advice they would give to the outsider wanting to help addicts, their answers would revolve around the same basic warning—don't get involved!

Almost all social and medical work today is based on non-involvement. The image of the ideal therapeutic worker or doctor has become one of a clinical and disinterested person who is extremely professional in approach and bearing, very precise, knowledgeable and kindly—but several places removed from the poor mortal in need of his help. The doctor's benevolent, even jovial, bedside manner or 'put you at ease' attitude in the surgery quickly turns to cooler professionalism when the bolder patient returns this apparent amity and tries to talk to him as a friend!

Voluntary workers engaged in counselling people with problems ranging from broken marriage to attempted suicide are frequently told by social help agencies that they must not become emotionally involved. They must simply befriend the person in need and be there to help him to think through his situation. If, for example, the problem is adultery, the counsellor must on no account become involved to the extent of making a value judgement on the matter. The tragedy is that many Christians faced with these situations find themselves torn between the rulings of their supervisors and the law of God, which uncompromisingly states: 'Thou shalt not commit adultery.'

Many nurses become distraught when they realise that patients need the kind of personal involvement and deep spiritual caring that they are not in a position to give. The probation service is no less burdened with this problem of involvement, perhaps even more so, precisely because the probation officer inevitably has to be more involved than others in an attempt to understand his client. I have a very profound respect for the service since most officers, although trained to be detached in relationships with clients, are men and women who know how to feel love for those they supervise and demonstrate a level of concern far beyond the call of duty. Were it not for the involvement of some probation officers many young addicts I have been able to help would be dead today, or still injecting, or in prison.

However, for the most part professional social workers remain faithful to their training—detached, clinical and uninvolved. This principle prevails throughout the public social services. The over-all structure of the professions precludes involvement. An internationally-known psychiatrist once said that the very nature of his profession made it impossible for him to come out from behind his desk and confess to his client that he really did care for him as a person. Instead he had to deal in words and sentiments which were strictly professional. He frankly admitted that he often longed for the opportunity to be involved, but his professional circumstances prevented him.

In saying this I do not want to be over-critical or cynical. But I feel it is important to establish the fact that non-involvement is a chief characteristic of nearly all present-day programmes, social, medical and psychiatric, which are directed at helping to cure the drug addict. There is some virtue in this, since over-involvement on the wrong levels could hinder the client and also cause unnecessary pain to the therapist, who might even become so burdened with the cares of his clients that he became a psychiatric patient himself. It is unfortunate, though, that professionalism has gone so far as to become almost a law and therefore a hindrance.

This book is written for Christian workers who believe that the answer to the drug addict's need is an encounter with the Lord Jesus Christ. What has been said so far about professional non-involvement contrasts strongly with what the Bible has to say. In getting through to drug addicts we need to be as fully involved as Christ was. We must be prepared to give ourselves completely. Yet if our involvement touches the emotional levels only, the result will be failure and we will become worthy of the criticisms made by professionals of untrained workers.

The biblical principle of involvement is aimed at introducing men to Jesus Christ, who alone can give the guilty conscience peace, and bring about that wonderful experience of new life described in 2 Corinthians 5:17—'If any man be in Christ, he is a new creature: old things are passed away; behold, all things are become new.'

In Acts 20:31 we see the perfect example of involved counselling. Paul, we read, counselled with tears. Most modern professional counsellors seem unable to cry or show any emotion, to register either shock or sorrow. But somehow it is hard to identify with another's heartbreak without shedding tears, or to help someone to come to terms with his wrong-doing without registering disapproval.

Sigmund Freud taught that 'ideally the analyst, as nearly as possible, must be a blank to the patient' (*Advances in Analytic-Therapy*, ed. Patrick Mullahy, 1967). Another analyst agreed by saying, 'one cornerstone of therapy has been that the therapist's personality must come into the picture as little as possible'. This view held that he should be a 'faceless mirror', essentially silent as a human being.

How stark is the contrast between this and the spirit of the prophet Jeremiah. Having warned the people of God to repent and humble themselves, Jeremiah says: 'But if ye will not hear it, my soul shall weep in secret places for your pride; and mine eye shall weep sore, and run down with tears, because the Lord's flock is carried away captive' (Jeremiah 13:17). The prophet was not ashamed to weep, as the Apostle Paul also wept for those he counselled and cared for. It would have been unthinkable for Paul to detach himself from those whom he had led to Christ or healed in the name of Jesus. He was involved physically, emotionally and spiritually with his world-wide flock.

Notice Paul's advice to his Christian brothers and sisters in 1 Corinthians 16:20. 'Greet ye one another with an holy kiss.' In this loveless and un-demonstrative age it is like a breath of fresh, heavenly air to see Christian people embracing one another, or laying a hand upon a shoulder instead of the formal, cold shake of the hand.

Our aim is to get through spiritually to the drug-taker, and indeed to all young people in need of the delivering power of the Gospel. This happens only when we, as Christian counsellors, can show love. Love is very costly. Paul sums it up in a chal-lenging statement to the Thessalonians (1 Thes-salonians 2:8): 'So being affectionately desirous of you, we were willing to have imparted unto you, not the gospel of God only, but also our own souls, because ye were dear unto us.'

The Gospel is not something vague and isolated; it is not a message which is indifferent or dis-passionate. It is the dynamic power of God, God's love, God's expression of a deep desire to be in-volved with His creation. Every time a counsellor tells the Gospel story he is using the most precious words and thoughts ever expressed. Every time I talk of God's great Calvary love, of the terrible death of His only Son on the Cross for me and my sins, I feel the emotion and the involvement of it. This is not the mere idealism and high-minded philosophy of an historic leader. This is the mes-sage of salvation for a lost and desperately wicked world—God's ultimate expression of love. God cannot be more deeply involved with us than at Calvary. Every Christian should feel an emotional response to the Cross.

Theology, the letter of the law, and orthodoxy are killing the spiritual life of many. The 'masses' reject Christianity because of its 'isms', its dogma and churchianity. Thousands of young people turn their backs on organised religion because it is cold and lifeless. Coming to Christ in repentance and with a sincere desire to turn from sin and follow God's way is a deep, emotionally thrilling experience. But because the modern intellectual Christian, evangelical or otherwise, has rationalised emotion out of conversion, the Holy Spirit also has become the subject of debate and argument and counter-argument. Believers who claim to be blessed by an experience of the Holy Spirit, whatever form it might take in the sovereignty of God, are judged unstable by their more 'mature' brethren and considered to be highly emotional and subjective, relying upon experience rather than doctrine.

In fact, 'experience' has become almost a shunned word among evangelicals. Many people I have counselled at our rehabilitation centre complain of the lifeless churches they find when they go back into the outside world. They say it is only because they know something better at this centre for one-time drug addicts that they are able to retain the joy of the Lord which they have found to be so real.

Having come into a thrilling relationship with Jesus Christ, they are disappointed to find a great lack of joy and free expression in so many churches. They find sombre organ voluntaries, smartly-dressed sidesmen with nothing to give away but a hymn book, and a rigid order of service.

Yes, the Word of God is preached. But the purpose of the Word is to lead us from bondage to liberty and life. The 'letter' is killing spiritual depth. The reason why so few young people are found in our churches today is not because the churches are not 'trendy' enough. There are plenty of those, sad to say! No, the real reason is a lack of genuine love and emotion and therefore little reality. Coldness of heart grows like a cancer in the land.

Paul was able to say that he had gone to the full loving lengths of real involvement. He could say not only that he had given the truth and power of God to the Thessalonians but also that he gave freely of himself. In giving himself he proved that Jesus was real, and that an experience with Jesus was reality. This was not a mere religion of laws he was offering, but love and abundant life.

It must be understood that many drug-users have experienced the false and unrewarding emotion of drugs. The drug-taker will argue that nothing can replace the warmth and pleasure and the illusion of security of the 'flash' or 'buzz' or the colours of a psychedelic trip. To the truly involved drug-taker, drugs are more important than girl friend, wife, children, home, ambition, wealth or position in life. Nothing has priority over his drug experience and he will sacrifice anything to get more drugs. Can a dull and lifeless religion match that?

I was once asked by a heroin addict what Christ could give him that 'H' could not. I replied: 'You will have me!' With Christ I offered him my friendship and loyalty, my love and the love of my family. When the euphoria of the drug experience

21

evaporated and left emptiness I would still be there. Paul says to the Corinthians concerning this deeply involved love which is part of the Christian experience: 'If you love someone you will be loyal to him no matter what the cost. You will . . . always stand your ground in defending him.' (1 Corinthians 13:7, Living Bible.) The same Apostle says in 1 Corinthians 9: 'To the weak became I as weak, that I might gain the weak: I am made all things to all men, that I might by all means save some. And this I do for the gospels' sake.

If you are ever to know what it means to get through to a drug-user or to see a young rebel change and relate to you, it will be only as he sees Jesus in you as perfectly as that, radiant with His wonderful compassion, purity and love. That will mean involvement on two levels. There is firstly involvement with Jesus—let Him melt your heart if it is hard and teach you to love as the angels love. And secondly there is involvement with the addict. He needs to know that you care enough to become involved at your own cost.

To a great extent Christians have neglected the power that is available to them through Christ to heal the apparently incurable mental sicknesses which are so common today. We have tended to leave such work to the 'specialists' of our day—psychologists, social workers, therapists and professional counsellors. The pastor has confined his counselling to straightforward 'spiritual' problems, or at the very outside to problems in marital and boy/girl relationships. He has not been consulted in problems of deep mental sickness and has unfortunately not presumed to take an active interest. In fact many psychiatrists have blamed the 'religion' of the client or patient for many mental problems.

In his book *Competent to Counsel*, Jay Adams quotes Professor O. Hobart Mowrer, who fearlessly states that current psychiatric dogmas are false and that modern psychiatry has failed. Mowrer believes that it is essential for people who are mentally sick because of guilt to confess their wrongs and face up to them. Jay Adams writes: 'There in those mental institutions, under Mowrer's methods, we began to see people labelled neurotic, psychotic and psychoneurotic helped by confessing deviant behaviour and assuming personal responsibility for it.' Mowrer, who has held the position of President of the American Psychological Association, asks in his book *The Crisis in Psychiatry and Religion:* 'Has evangelical religion sold its birthright for a mess of psychological potage?' What a challenge to Christians! The Church has abdicated its responsibility in the field of healing of the mind and left others, who know nothing of the healing power of Christ, to try to give the guilty conscience peace.

If you care for a young drug-user and truly want to see him healed, you can see a miracle take place in his life, but it will cost you full involvement with him on every level. If your concern is just a passing fancy, don't try to help an addict for he will demand your time and dedication and the sacrifice of your private life. The Christian has all the resources in Christ to heal a person whose mind is deeply scarred by the perpetual abuse of drugs and the false ideas that drug misuse has produced in

23

him. The statements of men like Mowrer prove that people are looking to Christians who fully believe in the mighty Word of God to take up the challenge to heal men and women in the name of Jesus.

Sometimes those of us who have been Christians for a few years forget the all-embracing joy of the change in our lives when we met Jesus and faced up to His claims. Anyone entering into a living relationship with Jesus literally becomes a new creation. Absolutely new! If we lose our joy we may even lose the ability to relate to those who don't know Christ and retire into an evangelical shell devoid of emotion and fearing involvement. Yet the prospect of a completely new life, a fresh start, is attractive and necessary to the young person whose life is dominated by drugs, who literally has to inject his own little bit of colour into a dull and aimless life.

A closer look at Paul's attitude to involvement leads us to 2 Corinthians 11:29, where he wrote: 'Who is weak, and I am not weak? who is offended, and I burn not?' Who was led into sin without Paul's intense, loving concern? As I have pointed out already, the professional counsellor is usually trained to maintain an attitude of neutrality in counselling, no matter what his personal feelings might be. For the Apostle this was impossible, as it ought to be for all those who seek to deal in depth with people in deep emotional and spiritual distress. Paul felt the weakness of those he cared for, not condoning them but stating clearly that he could not feel at ease or have any joy within while his children were falling into weaknesses of the flesh. He could not sit down with someone who had committed some sinful act or fallen into crime and allow them to talk their heads off, doing nothing but supplying an ear. Paul could not be the neutral counsellor. He wept over weakness and rebuked sin. He placed his finger on the hurtful spot and left the one in need in no doubt as to what he thought of his foolishness. If I talk to an addict or any young person in need through his or her own sinfulness, I show concerned love which rebukes them for what is wrong. That is involvement. It demands tears and sleepless nights—but repays with great victory.

'I have no greater joy than to hear that my children walk in truth,' writes John (3 John 1:4). When someone in need rejects counsel, the trained and disinterested counsellor will simply shrug his shoulders and consider the matter closed. The involved Christian counsellor can only feel sorrow when the one he cares for rejects a course he knows would save him.

Finally, let's look at two of the main aspects of Paul's involvement—its purpose and its nature.

Its purpose was to bring men to Christ and into a deeper understanding of what it meant to follow Christ and to obey His Word. Its ultimate goal was to glorify God by producing men of God who were fully committed to Him. Paul's lifelong desire was to see men not only saved from sin but living God-glorifying lives in love, holiness and obedience. Paul was not concerned with mere human ties, but with eternal commitment to the glory of the Eternal God.

Its nature was complete human and spiritual involvement inspired by the love of God. It was not the transient love of the human heart. The professional is right to guard against emotional involvement alone, for that is dangerous. The love of the spiritual counsellor will fail if it is only sentimental. His must be the *agape* love of 1 Corinthians 13—long-suffering, kind, gentle, patient, Christlike, warm. If you cannot show love for someone without wanting to receive some human emotional benefit, then this work is not for you. The kind of involvement demanded is summed up in these qualities:

an ability to stick with the one seeking help no matter what the cost;

a tender-hearted concern which can be shown in tears and love;

a passionate desire to see souls saved;

an *agape* kind of love;

patience and tactfulness;

an ability not to be upset by the testing attacks of the one you are trying to help;

a willingness to cast all cares upon the Lord when the situation seems impossible.

The last point mentioned is the safety valve of Christian involvement. The secular counsellor has no power outside the professional training he has been given and the advice of his superiors. But the spiritual counsellor has a wealth of divine power. When, with all the sincerity of real involvement, he has tried and failed to get through to the addict, in desperate need he can turn in prayer to the One whose servant he really is and confess: 'Lord I have failed—but You never fail. I entrust this soul to you.' It is true that many miracles have taken place in the lives of addicts when a worker has given up and asked the Lord to take over.

Remember, give yourself as you give the Gospel. Never give yourself alone, for you can do nothing. Many, many reading this weep tears unashamedly for those whom they seek to win and may God reward the one who weeps with the joy of a great harvest of souls.

2 / Addict means slave

In simple terms there is only one kind of drug addict—the person who has taken addictive substances such as heroin, methedrine, morphine or cocaine over a period of several weeks, building up a physical and mental tolerance to the drug and a dependence upon it. The word 'addict' suggests a 'dependent' or 'slave'. In Holland the word that is used for a drug addict is *veslafden*, which literally means 'slave'.

A first excursion into the narcotic dreamland is often by sniffing or inhaling powdered heroin, sometimes known as 'snorting horse'. The experimenter graduates to 'skin popping'—intramuscular injection of the drug, pushing the needle of the syringe into the surface of the skin. Since with this method the effect takes time to build up and the 'flash point' of the experience is therefore dissipated, it is not long before a desire for greater satisfaction persuades the addict to start 'mainlining'—injecting into the vein.

From this stage on the addict is in a state of chronic addiction, with which develop several frightening physical and mental side-effects. If deprived of his drugs an addict will become the victim of terrible mental and physical pain, both real and imagined. In extreme cases, where no medical aid is available, addicts have been known to die while going through this withdrawal period. Some have suffocated to death on their own vomit.

The person who has turned to drugs is often

searching desperately for the kind of dynamic experience only to be discovered in a living relationship with Jesus Christ. Many addicts are looking for the satisfaction that is found only in the peace and joy of knowing Jesus as Lord.

While understanding all this, the Christian should also be careful to arm himself adequately with real wisdom and practical knowledge of the drug problem before he attempts to rush off into the streets to reach addicts. The Christian who wants to communicate the love of God to addicts with any degree of convicting power must understand that drug addiction is an extremely complex social problem, and that some knowledge of the factors involved is essential.

My own ministry to drug addicts began with a call from God which was followed hard by a realisation that I must equip myself with knowledge. And in 1965 I began to work under a very skilled psychiatrist in a South London mental hospital, where I learned some very valuable things.

Getting through to the young drug addict has for many years been an insoluble problem in the eyes of the most experienced of psychiatrists and professional counsellors. It is not that the extensive medical and psychiatric treatments they devise prove ineffective, but rather that the after-care of addicts is virtually non-existent and so the rate of relapse is appallingly high. The Christian worker among addicts should be conversant with current treatment trends and understand where and why they fail.

Let us first understand that there is a great deal of difference between the drug-user and the addict.

Experimenting with pills or smoking 'pot' (marijuana) does not constitute addiction. Addiction involves the kind of craving which is satisfied only by increasingly large doses at more and more frequent intervals. Thousands of today's young people take pills and smoke pot without becoming addicts, although these actions are often preliminary steps in a life of dependence on drugs.

A useful definition of the term 'addict' was given by a World Health Organisation committee in 1957. Drug addiction, their report states, 'is a state of periodic or chronic intoxication produced by the repeated consumption of a drug, natural or synthetic'. The report listed four essential components of addiction—an overpowering desire or need, a tendency to increase the dose, a psychological, and generally a physical, dependence on the effect of the drug, and a detrimental effect on the individual and on society.

Drug habituation, on the other hand, is a condition 'resulting from the repeated consumption of a drug'. This is characterised by a desire, but not a compulsion, to continue taking the drug for the sense of well-being it gives, little or no tendency to increase the dose, some degree of psychological dependence but an absence of physical dependence, and detrimental effects, if any, only to the individual.

In 1964 the World Health Organisation recommended that the term 'drug dependence' be substituted for the earlier terms 'addiction' and 'habituation'.

'Drug dependence is a state of psychic and physical dependence, or both, on a drug, arising in

30

a person following administration of that drug on a continuous basis. The characteristics of such a state will vary with the agent involved, and these characteristics must always be made clear by designating the particular type of drug dependence in each specific case: for example, drug dependence of morphine type, of barbiturate type, etc.'

Apart from the use of strongly addictive drugs, the abuse of barbiturates and pills constitutes a rapidly growing problem in its own right, as does the increasing number of users of 'delirients', who compulsively 'sniff' or inhale from various solvents and chemicals. It is doubtful whether there is a school in the country that does not have its group of drug-takers. But these types of drug-abusers cannot be classed as addicts in the strictest medical and social terms. So let us get our terminology right before we tackle the problem. There is a very real danger in foolish and unqualified statements, however well-meaning.

In Britain drug addicts have always been considered sick people, with addiction as their disease—an attitude which contrasts strongly with views held in other parts of Europe and the United States. In the States, where there is an enormous drug problem, addicts are looked on as criminals. Their dependence is their crime.

The cultural and social background of the American addict is so different from that of the European addict that we must view the problem entirely separately. And since a great deal of literature has been produced about *American* drug addiction, it is as well to remember that what is said in it cannot be applied directly to dealing with addicts in other countries.

There are a number of characteristics which distinguish drug addicts in this country from addicts in the United States. Until 1967 most addicts in Britain received drugs under the National Health Service and under strict medical supervision. In the States, addicts are supplied by 'pushers' who buy drugs in bulk quantities from large and well established criminal organisations. Because the drugs are obtained illegally they are substandard, often manufactured in 'underground' laboratories and mixed with all kinds of impurities.

Although criminal activities are part of the life of almost every drug addict, Britain's attitude has been that the addict is first and foremost in need of medical help rather than punishment. This humane view would seem to have been very wise since the situation in Britain has continued to be more controlled and drug addiction less involved with the criminal scene than in other countries.

The situation has changed slightly in recent years, following claims that the freedom exercised by general practitioners in prescribing drugs under the National Health Service was contributing to a rise in addiction. A few doctors were subjected to a great deal of adverse publicity after it was discovered that they had been over-prescribing for young addicts for material gain. These addicts were selling their surplus to others who were not officially registered to receive drugs.

So, in 1967, the British government took the prescribing of the drugs concerned out of the hands of local doctors and set up treatment centres attached to hospitals in large towns and cities. At these centres psychiatrists, social workers and other professional workers provide help for addicts. This system means that there is much stricter control over the distribution of drugs.

But, since the setting up of these centres, there has also been a steady increase in Britain of illegal trafficking in drugs. There is now a growing black market dealing in drugs, especially in 'Chinese heroin' from Hong Kong, a deadly drug containing many impurities. Whether this is a natural trend aggravated by the 1967 Act or whether it was more directly caused by it is hard to say. The authorities are doing a great deal to try to halt the problem—mostly in vain. It is only as we look beyond man that we can find a solution to this distressing problem.

3 / Get knowledge

I believe in the power of the Gospel to set drug addicts free and in the power of the Holy Spirit to keep them free. I am utterly convinced that the spiritual approach to the drug problem is the only really lasting cure because it deals with the cause and not the effects.

The Christian who shares these views must face up to the fact that there are many doctors, psychiatrists, social workers and voluntary agencies equally convinced that their own approach is the right one. If this was not so they would not be so deeply involved in caring. In many ways the non-Christian worker contributes powerfully on levels of involvement and real human love which are rarely shown these days.

Many zealous Christians often unthinkingly dismiss these secular workers out of hand, but I feel that such zeal is not based on knowledge—the failing which Paul discovered in the Jews and wrote of in Romans 10. I have been appalled by the almost bigoted lack of knowledge of the simple, basic medical or sociological aspects of the drug problem with which many Christians are content.

Before we attempt to help addicts we must understand, as fully as it is possible for laymen to understand, the reasons why a person uses drugs. Before we dare to offer a spiritual answer we must understand the deep longing of those who turn to drugs. It is one thing to assert that Christ is the answer—another to understand what he is the answer to! In other words, while we understand the answer, we seldom grasp the question.

Doctors and other professionals who have spent many years becoming highly qualified in their careers find it very hard to accept the untrained and uninformed Christian worker—especially if that person hasn't even the simple courtesy to admit that he doesn't have all the answers! God has all the answers, but His people are ever learning and cannot claim to know the Lord's mind completely.

My own ministry among drug addicts led, in 1967, to the setting up of our residential rehabilitation centre in the heart of the Gloucestershire countryside for the Christian treatment of young addicts. The whole concept of the work of Life for the World revolves around the sure knowledge that Jesus Christ in His agonising death on a cross gave the guilty conscience freedom. He can heal and completely restore the drug addict as He can deliver any soul in need.

In these truths lie the only ultimate cure for the drug addict. The knowledge of this cure is a tremendous responsibility for any Christian. It can, however, be effectively nullified by our wrong handling of it in an ignorant approach to drug addicts. Dramatic promises and big claims on behalf of the Lord are often fruitless. It is more difficult but infinitely more worth-while to aim for deep, long-lasting work in the heart of an addict.

Professor Isador Chein, an eminent American psychologist, has said that there are three distinguishing factors in the making of an addict, which combined produce chronic addiction. It is essential to understand this, for it will help us in presenting the Gospel and in knowing not only how to offer Jesus, but why. The three factors are a pre-disposing psychological inadequacy (or, more simply, a weak personality), a crisis of some kind and a timely offer of drugs.

The world in which we live produces some very inadequate personalities. Certainly, in that the Bible states that all have sinned and fallen short of God's glory, all mankind is spiritually inadequate. But there are many other issues involved which can give rise to dissatisfaction with life in general. And it is dissatisfaction working on a weak personality which is the first factor in the making of an addict.

The second factor, the crisis, is more variable. It could be a quarrel with a girl friend, an examination failure, the death of a parent. Often a great crisis of loneliness will prompt a person to turn to drugs.

The third factor, the timely offer of drugs, is often present these days because so many young people experiment with drugs that there is almost always a place in the neighbourhood where drugs are known to be available. When the first two factors are in operation the third usually follows on quickly.

Just as there are three factors which lead to an initial use of drugs, so it is generally accepted that there are three stages through which a user progresses to addiction. There is firstly the mental inclination towards drugs, secondly the physical experimentation and thirdly the psychological and physical dependence on drugs.

The drug-user you meet could be at any one of these stages. There are always thousands of young people at the first stage, mentally aligned to drugs and potentially in danger of addiction. Such a person may be merely thinking sympathetically about drugs and drug experiences. He will perhaps discuss drugs and agree with drug-users that soft drugs such as cannabis should be legalised. He may never have taken drugs, but his mental inclination could easily lead him to the next step.

A first fix cannot be physically addicting, but it does leave a definite desire to experiment further and often gives the user that feeling of well-being, the coveted 'high' or sense of euphoria. The actual 'buzz' or 'flash' referred to by addicts happens in the section of the brain above the ear and in fact lasts for only a split second. It is followed by a sensation of floating on a bed of cotton-wool which lets you very gently down to earth. Because the user has injected drugs into his body only intramuscularly, he is persuaded to think that he can safely use more.

It is true that it is no great problem for a doctor to withdraw even the most hardened addict from drugs. But a great many wrong statements have been made about the subject of withdrawal in the past. Many Christians mistakenly believe that it is easy to remove an addict from drugs by 'cold turkey'—complete alienation from drugs without medical assistance. The attitude is often that, if drugs are suddenly removed, the Lord will sustain the addict through the withdrawal. This is an attitude of blind incomprehension rather than a complete confidence in a miracle-working God!

I remember a case of this in London, when a group of zealous Christians brought a young addict in off the street. He had been using three grains of heroin a day as well as other drugs. He was a very sick boy, but in a toxic state had agreed to go with the Christians. The group really did care about him and believed that God would heal him. After praying over him for some time, they took away his drugs and fixing equipment and destroyed them. They were certainly not prepared for what followed. The boy's vomit soon covered the bed. He shook all over and continually cried out in great pain. He became violent and excreted. Finally he fell into a state of deep unconsciousness from which no amount of shaking, shouting or praying could awaken him. At last an ambulance was called and the boy's life was saved. A little longer and he would certainly have died. Many addicts have died in withdrawal. It is a very dangerous thing to encourage anyone to go 'cold turkey' without medical advice.

If you hear examples of patients in the United States going through 'cold turkey' with no ill effects it is because the American addict is using drugs which are far more impure than those used by his counterpart in Britain. British addicts are more seriously addicted than American addicts. A registered British addict may be consuming an average of up to twenty times as much pure heroin a day as an American addict.

It is short-sighted to assume that this kind of knowledge is unnecessary in approaching addicts. I would seriously question the genuineness of a person's desire to help addicts if he was not pre-

38

pared to learn about their problem. After all, there are thousands of other young people not using drugs but in equal need of Jesus Christ. It is better to spend your time with them than superficially to cut corners in work with drug addicts or users. Let your zeal be deepened by knowledge!

4 / A time for everything

The soundest advice in the whole world is to be found in the Bible, including advice on the subject of counselling. As Christian counsellors we should approach those addicted to drugs or under the influence of drugs with great care. There is a right and a wrong time for everything, as we are told in the book of Ecclesiastes. In particular there is a time to speak and a time to be silent.

The principle of silence is one found often in the Scriptures and therefore worthy of more than a brief consideration. Recent generations of evangelical Christians have been brought up in an atmosphere of intense and aggressive evangelism. It is repeated over and over again that it is vital not to lose an opportunity to witness for Jesus Christ, putting aside all personal inconvenience. This concept is one which I wholeheartedly believe and teach. But there is much more to being a witness for Christ than 'sounding off' at any poor sinner man who happens to pass! There is, for example, the witness of the daily life of the committed Christian. There is being where you are needed, doing the right thing, avoiding following the crowd—there are so many practical acts which can be a powerful witness. It is effective to show to others that the daily Christian life is satisfying, joyful and a dramatic contrast with the grey drabness of the world around. It is as important to know when not to speak as when to do so.

Let me quote an illustration of this. John, a keen worker in his local church, was anxious to do more for the young people in the central area of the town where the church was situated. As a form of evangelistic outreach, he planned a coffee bar to draw in young drifters and drug-users. The coffee bar opened and established itself quickly, attracting crowds every Saturday night. One group of young people who often came in were recognised as drug-takers. John and his friends, in spite of not knowing what drugs the group were using or to what extent, sallied forth with much enthusiasm to win them for Christ. They were soon deeply involved in conversation. John was pleasantly surprised to find that these young people were not only interested in talking about religion but they appeared to know a great deal about it! They had obviously studied many religions, including Christianity. Thrilled by this, John pressed home to them the most urgent Gospel truths. But suddenly one of the drug-users announced dramatically: 'I've met Jesus Christ!'

'Do you mean you know Christ, then?' asked one of John's friends, visibly registering reverence and respect for this young man . . .

'Oh, yes, I know him all right. We often talk together about all kinds of things,' came back the confident reply.

'Do you love Him?' asked John, a little nervously. 'I mean, have you trusted Christ as Saviour and Lord?' he went on, feeling on more firm evangelical ground.

Back came the uncompromising reply. 'I don't know about that, but I do know I've seen Jesus Christ. And heard the most lovely music.'

Poor John could hardly bear it. 'But what

church do you go to?' The reply from all was the same: 'None!'

Writing in the church magazine to report on the progress of the coffee bar, John told of the young people who had come along and found Christ, or at least had seen Him. They were a little unorthodox, but they knew Christ. At least, he was almost sure they did!

In fact the young people in question knew nothing of the experience of a spiritual rebirth, but rather the empty counterfeit experience of the drug LSD. Their visions of Christ were among a whole company of hallucinatory experiences. John had rushed in without really listening or learning. Many addicts profess religious visions after taking hallucinatory drugs. I met one young man who was convinced that he had met Christ and had been on a trip to heaven under the influence of cocaine. He was further convinced, having studied the Bible, that the writer of the Revelation, John the Divine, was a cocaine addict or was under the influence of some drug to have experienced what he did!

Our young Christian worker John had mistakenly assumed that the young people coming to his coffee bar were having normal experiences. Knowing nothing about the effects of addiction, he was not prepared for the possibility that the experiences they related were drug-induced and therefore not genuine. Thousands of young people in the world today are spiritually minded, but that does not make them Christians. Many addicts believe that the hallucinogenic substances they take open their minds to a new spiritual dimension.

This attitude, I believe, reflects a universal hunger for God and reality. But the satisfaction offered by drugs is artificial.

'What can Christ give me that drugs don't already give me?' This challenge is often heard and is not easy to answer. Many drug-users are dedicated to their drugs and the drug subculture way of life. A Christian wishing to communicate the message that a life with Christ is truly more full must not rush into a situation unprepared, but must always listen before talking. Listen with care and try to understand the addict, even though it is difficult sometimes to remain silent, with such a wonderful story to tell.

A great deal of evangelism is carried out in the central areas of large cities, such as Soho in London. The young people wandering around the streets there are looking for drugs and a 'good time', and not knowingly looking for God. The best approach is just to let an addict know that you are someone willing to help him if he gets into trouble. It is futile to present the whole counsel of God to someone who is not even searching for Him. Often a Christian witnessing in the streets will find a sympathetic ear from an addict under the influence of drugs or even in a state of acute intoxication or narcosis. But when the addict returns to a less stupified state, he will have little or no recollection of what has happened to him or been said to him.

In the early days of my work among drug addicts in London, I talked to scores of addicts queueing outside the all-night chemist's shop in Piccadilly Circus. Some, entirely preoccupied with the thought of the next fix, were deaf to my words. Others would listen and agree with what I said, even give me their addresses and ask me to call on them. But when I arrived on their doorsteps the next day they did not recognise me.

Real, genuine thought is not possible to the person under the influence of heroin, barbiturates or cannabis in certain forms. Though he may appear to be in full possession of his senses the addict does not absorb anything into his heart. I have learned that in these circumstances it is best to show an addict friendship and understanding, but to reserve the good news of the Gospel until he is better able to pay attention to things that matter.

Find out how old he is, where he lives, what drugs he is using. Develop a sanctified ability to listen, and in doing so you can learn how to approach a drug-user with the greatest effect. The golden rule when counselling addicts is to wait for the right time of need to step in with the Gospel.

When Jesus arrived in a city or town, he would visit the places where the common people gathered. He sat with drunkards and prostitutes, with the criminals and drop-outs of the day. Our Lord didn't need to do a lot of talking. His presence was enough. I'm sure He spent hours with those inadequate and needy people, listening to them and understanding their needs, showing that He was prepared to be deeply involved with them. It was only after working among drug addicts for three years that I felt I knew enough about their problems really to propose an answer.

There is also a very Scriptural reason for taking

44

care when we speak. The Lord warned against preaching the Gospel to those who are not ready or willing to listen, who treat the word of God like rubbish, trampling on the pearls of God's wisdom like pigs trampling over swill. Don't debase the precious truths of the Gospel by speaking about them in the wrong context, at the wrong time. If words which tell of eternal life and holiness sound unimportant or trivial it will be twice as difficult for the addict to listen the next time. When you talk to an addict under the influence of his drugs you are reaching only his outer ear. You are not contacting his mind or his heart.

In saying this I do not overlook the power of God's Holy Spirit to break through all barriers. I believe that it is possible for a man to believe in Christ without a complete mental understanding and acceptance, but when the Holy Spirit breaks through everyone involved will know about it. The Christian is offering a wonderful, life-giving message. He must be sure to take his time in getting through to the addict with the whole message.

5 / The professionals

From the start of my work among addicts in London I felt that the Lord wanted me to contact addicts under treatment and to co-operate with the doctors involved in order to learn how best to help.

My conviction about this was tested by the frightening early experiences I had with professionals in the field of drug addiction. Being interviewed for the first time by a very skilled psychiatrist in one of the country's largest mental institutions, where there were many heroin addicts under treatment, my heart sank as he pronounced me 'yet another do-gooder'. I was advised to abandon a useless task. Professionals often see people from outside who want to help as nuisances, as 'do-gooders'—tags that will stick with us until we prove otherwise.

I was determined not to be put off and to prove that I was useful. And it was only as I began to get close to addicts in that hospital that I began to realise in exactly what ways I could be of use. The wonderful news of Jesus and His love is a precious gift to anyone. But these addicts needed the power of Christ in action, in the actions of the Christian. They needed something very tangible, like someone to get personally involved with them, to find them a home, a job, a bed, to visit a worried mother or father.

In the first three years of my work with addicts, I concentrated on learning from doctors and social workers in mental hospitals. Eagerness to learn opened many doors for me, so that I was able to join in all the hospital activities and attend lectures in psychology and psychiatric medicine. In my dealings with doctors I found it important to recognise that they knew much about the mental state of the patient, even though I knew something about the spiritual. So many Christians make the basic mistake of feeling that if they give credit to a psychiatrist for having some knowledge of the unconscious mind they might be compromising their own convictions. This is both foolish and unnecessary. God can heal the sickness of the addict's mind, but it is helpful to know from doctors just what form that sickness is taking. Psychologists and psychiatrists are often dismissed as the poor relations of the medical profession. But many that I know within these professions are skilled and sensitive men and women who are themselves searching for answers to life's questions.

I believe that Jesus who knew, as the Bible tells us, 'what was in man', far surpassed today's psychologists in understanding. His methods of treating people in need brought about a real healing of the mind.

Study the story of the woman taken in adultery. Jesus first dealt with the crowd around her, challenging: 'Let him that is without sin cast the first stone.' Here was a man who knew the hearts of the people. Having dealt with the problems around, Jesus was then able to turn to the woman, asking her if there was anyone to condemn her. 'None,' she replied, and Jesus sent her away, saying 'Neither do I condemn you, go and sin no more.' It was simple spiritual therapy of biblical psychology.

The aim is to deal first with the opposition. With a drug addict this means finding out what is causing him to turn to drugs or to remain on drugs. Doctors are often very willing and able to help with this aspect of the problem.

Notice how Jesus dealt with all kinds of people—the prostitute, the drunkard, the robber, the leper, the madman possessed of evil spirits. He did not waste his words. It is very psychologically sound to say little, to listen and then to weigh your words very carefully.

Notice also how Jesus dealt with His own followers, His disciples. He called to be with Him men from all walks of life, with all kinds of temperaments and personal problems, seeing always their potential. In Simon, the bluff and clumsy fisherman, He saw Peter, the Rock. In Saul, the persecutor, He saw Paul, the great and beloved Apostle. Jesus showed in His dealings with men and women a deep and sensitive understanding of them. If we are to follow the Lord's example, we should look beyond the mere appearance of people and glimpse a vision of their potential.

When working alongside professionals, learn what their treatments and techniques are before you make sweeping condemnatory statements. Often there is something useful to be learned. There are many, many openings that a doctor can give you which are otherwise unobtainable, such as entry to hospitals. The most needy and chronic cases of drug addiction are to be found in hospitals all over the country. Lying in a hospital bed, the addict often comes to a realisation of how false the drug world is. He is perhaps searching for something to fill the great vacuum he has tried to satisfy with drugs. This is often the stage when a word of witness will bring conviction to his heart.

If you are interested in the opportunities for witness in this way, offer your help as a visitor to the doctor in charge of your nearest treatment centre. Don't be afraid to become involved with the professionals. If your convictions are shaken by such involvement then you should not be attempting to counsel addicts at all!

6 / Getting through

Some years ago a psychiatrist told me that to cure the addict fully the doctor needed to change the addict's personality. He described it like this: 'If only it were possible to invade the inner man, to touch the hidden depths of the mind or spirit, we would find a cure, not only to drug addiction, but to the many other perplexing mental illnesses which defy all attempts at being healed.'

It was challenging for me to hear these words being voiced by such a skilled man. For I knew that the Christian message was able to effect just this kind of dramatic change in a man. In my work among doctors, psychiatrists, prison workers and others I have heard many express this same wish—if only there was something to reach and revolutionise the inner depths of a man! And some are now beginning to realise that the Christian approach is promoting the kind of treatment which does change lives.

The addict, in spite of all his particular barriers, is possessed of the same hungry and thirsty soul as any man, and no psychiatrist on earth can reach it. When we talk about getting through we mean reaching the deepest part of the human heart, the inner man that longs for life. The addict is like any other when it comes to the pressing need for freedom from guilt, from sin, from self. Jesus died for sinners, and addicts are sinners. They need to hear the same Gospel as any needy soul.

While realising the power of the Gospel, I continue to work alongside medical men and psychiatrists. One of the main reasons is that many professionals, although cynical, are prepared to accept that voluntary workers and Christians in particular have a vital contribution to make on this deep level of reaching and changing the inner man. Drug addiction is not like cancer or tuberculosis. It is principally a disease of the mind and heart. The Christian message is a powerful therapeutic tool in the work of curing drug addicts, but often the mistake is made of acting prematurely and without medical advice where it is needed. I have seen miracles take place where addicts seriously dependent on drugs have been set free in a very short time, but I have seen many, many more come through the hard way. So both caution and medical assistance should be wisely used in the early days of rehabilitating the addict.

I know a God who is a worker of miracles, who can heal the sick and do amazing things in these days. I believe the Holy Spirit is being poured out in these days as in the Acts of the Apostles. But I still advise caution in dealing with the addict. Counselling anyone is a serious business, but getting through to the addict is an extremely difficult task.

The zealous, faithful friend eager to go out and lay hands on an addict may well be greatly disappointed. I have seen and known enthusiastic Christians meeting addicts to pray over them, lay hands on them and weep for them, and do all manner of things to get them to give up drugs. They have given clothes, food, money, opened homes, in an attempt to see the power of Christ revealed in the young lives for which they are so desperately concerned.

Sadly, there are today many addicts in London who will tell you how they have testified to God in meetings, even 'spoken in tongues'. And all the time they have been laughing up their sleeves at the gullibility of misguided Christian friends.

Total lack of morality is one of the main characteristics of the drug world. Addicts will lie persistently in order to obtain money falsely and get sympathy. They will quite happily throw their drugs into the nearest dustbin if they know they can 'con' someone out of a fiver. The addict has no intention of giving up drugs; he will simply be able to buy even more with the money he has gained by his hard luck story and feigned repentance. Promises are nothing to the addict.

Often a group of Christians have taken an addict into their home and been really convinced that God was working miracles in his life. Perhaps he testifies in meetings or prays aloud. He is given new clothes and becomes a local celebrity. Then it is discovered that he is still an addict, he is secretly getting drugs regularly from a clinic. His whole life is a lie.

This is normal behaviour for the addict and the Christian worker must be prepared for it. Even after an addict has been at a rehabilitation centre for some time the old habit of lying comes back with the ease of much familiarity. It is important to ensure that an addict is held back from testifying or speaking publicly until there is real evidence to prove that he will be sincere and not tempted to put on a big act for the crowd. There is no reason why a converted addict is any more special than a converted anyone else, and care should be taken not to make him the centre of all attention. It is important to do as much as possible to prevent a young addict from lying to you or taking advantage of you as he might become hardened against a real sense of the presence of God when it comes. In this work precious lives are hanging in the balance.

Getting through to an addict is an urgent task, but it is not one to be rushed into. Take time to get to know him in a simple, unassuming and friendly manner. Let him know that you care about him as a person. Never give him cause to think that you just want him to swell your church membership or to put a feather in your spiritual cap. He will initially be touched only by a genuine concern. The addict is used to an attitude of clinical disinterest from others to whom he is just another depressing statistic. Be different. Be the love of Christ to him.

Remember that an addict has no real friends. The one he calls 'friend' is most likely to be the person who keeps him well supplied with drugs. Friendship conveys little to him. And if you are not consistent in your friendship he will quickly forget you. So you must be prepared to be involved. Be reliable, stay close to him. Addicts have been known to take overdoses and die when someone they have learned to rely on fails to turn up.

It is a mistake, too, to rush an addict off to the nearest evangelistic service. He won't understand it. It is far better to tell him in very simple terms about your own experience. Tell him what Christ means to you and how He has changed you. Spend time showing the love of Christ, and wait patiently for a response. Preach the Gospel clearly and confidently.

Remember to use knowledge. If the addict you are befriending continues to use drugs go with him when he goes for his prescriptions to the doctor or treatment centre. Find out how heavily he is addicted and to what drugs. Talk with his doctor. Find out if he really wants to give up drugs. Most addicts do want to give up drugs, but many won't admit it. If he appears sincerely to want to give up drugs suggest that he goes to a hospital for withdrawal. If he is disillusioned by the failure of previous treatments assure him that with Christ all things are possible, so this time it really could work. Tell him that after hospital treatment he could go to a Christian rehabilitation centre.

In all this study your Bible constantly and be ready to answer any challenges the addict may throw at you. One challenge you may often be faced with is: 'You say Christ has an answer for everything, but what does He know about being an addict?' If you know your Bible you will know the full extent of Christ's experiences. You will be able to tell the addict that when Jesus hung upon the cross He was bearing the sin of the whole world—past, present and future. He felt in His body all the hurt and anguish of sin, all the filth of the world, the brutality, the horror, the crime of mankind. He took it all upon Himself, even the needle marks of the addict. Jesus suffered more horribly than any drug addict. 'He was wounded for our transgressions. And by His stripes we are healed.'

The real miracle in the work of reclaiming these young lives is not in getting them off their drugs, but in keeping them off. In order to withstand the strong pull of drugs and his drug-orientated existence an addict must change his direction in life. Usually it takes time for him to learn to live without the prop of drugs and, as the Scriptures put it, to grow in grace. The work of the Christian begins in earnest when the doctor has withdrawn the addict from drugs. It is then that the Gospel can be applied to his life like a healing balm. The message of Christ and His love then begins to satisfy, to fill the vacuum once so poorly and inadequately occupied by drugs.

The Gospel is powerful because it changes lives. It gives hope and freedom from guilt. Former addicts who have come to know Jesus as Lord and Master of their lives recognise that their experimentation with drugs resulted from an inner spiritual hunger which wanted satisfaction. The doctor can restore the body; only the Holy Spirit can regenerate the heart.

In work among addicts it is wiser not to work alone. If you have a sympathetic minister or vicar tell him about the person you are counselling and ask his advice.

There is one final word of caution. Because addicts are people with complex psychological and spiritual problems an addict may hurt you and reject all that you do or say. After listening to you and even apparently accepting all you say for weeks or even months, he may completely turn against you for no obvious reason. You must be prepared for this. If you possibly can, keep in touch with him. This may be the time when he needs you most. He may even be testing you to see how genuine your concern for him is.

In all your dealings with drug addicts you will need to keep very near to the Lord. Pray daily and for long periods for the person laid on your heart. Pray for wisdom, courage and steadfastness. Remember that you are nothing and cannot save a soul. But Jesus can use you when you are fully yielded to Him and it is He who saves souls. Don't attempt to heal the addict in your own strength; it's impossible. Trust in the Holy Spirit to undertake. That's when the miracles start to happen!

7 / Residential rehabilitation

Because of the enormous temptations for the addict in his drug-centred environment, I believe that rehabilitation is most effectively tackled when the addict is physically distant from his old familiar surroundings. Any treatment centre in London or other large city, for example, has to fight continually against the strong lures provided by the nearby streets and alleyways. These constantly remind the patient of his drugs and his addicted friends, the places where he met his 'pusher', the street corners and cafés where he would meet other addicts and talk of nothing but drugs, the underground stations and public conveniences where he would inject, where he would hide, where he would be sick after a bad dose.

Addicts have many complex problems that the street worker will probably never encounter. In a residential setting these very deep-rooted problems surface and have to be solved.

Addicts come to the Life for the World centre at Northwick Park through contacts with probation officers or doctors or through our own work in London. After applying for a place, an addict is invited to come for a day's interview. His first reactions to our centre itself, to the staff and to the other boys in residence who have come to know the Lord and found in Him freedom from drugs, are vital and make a great deal of difference to our decision as to whether to accept him or not. We are looking for a sense of need and a desire to come off drugs in the prospective resident, even if these things are covered up with cynicism, fear, ambivalence, awkwardness or a dozen other fronts with which he may hide the real person.

A senior resident will be given the responsibility of showing the addict round the house and explaining the rules. These are tough, but based on experience. A willingness to keep the rules displays a genuine desire to be rid of addiction. The rules include:

No visitors for six weeks
No phone calls
No smoking
No breaking of bounds
Bed by 11 p.m.
Work from 9 a.m. to 5.30 p.m.

Yes, the rules *are* hard, especially on the life that has run wilfully wild. The addict has, in a misguided search for 'freedom', abandoned laws, moral codes, rules and regulations—and is a failure. Centres with little discipline show few results. At Northwick Park there is a lot of discipline, but all rules are purposeful and based on the love and law of God.

Many of the mistakes that young people make are because somewhere, somehow they lost control. When faced with temptation, such as drugtaking, they were unable to make a controlled and sound decision. Before the addict can ever face the world without drugs and be able to resist its many demands, he must firstly be able to face up to himself and to say 'no' to self when it wants its own way.

The Christian emphasis of Life for the World is laid before the applicant at the same time as the rules. We make it clear that we know of only one way in which we can help, although others offer different ways. We offer Jesus and the promises of God, and tell the addict plainly that a rejection of the old life and a fresh start will work only within the experience of a spiritual 'rebirth'. And an addict must positively feel that Northwick Park can help him before he becomes a resident.

The moment he arrives the newcomer is made to feel part of a family and a community all at the same time. In the Northwick family he experiences the love of others and the security which that love gives. The community spirit provides a basis for discipline and he is expected to contribute to the community from the start. Each resident has to give one hour's cleaning service each day before going to his work programme. This may be in the house—plumbing, carpentry, decorating, electrical work—or it may be in the kitchen, the market garden, the farm or the printing press. With few exceptions there is a spirit of industry as these young men, many of whom have never held a steady job down, contribute to the general good of the community in their work.

The power of the spiritual life of the centre can be seen in many ways. After a few weeks with the help of counselling, example and prayer, old habits begin to lose their control and attitudes change. Since Northwick Park opened its doors to young addicts in 1968 about 150 have lived there, many of them seriously searching for truth and reality. Today many ex-residents, once hopelessly addicted to heroin or confused to the brink of insanity by LSD, are working as printers, gardeners, cooks, hotel managers, office workers. One is a film actor, two are at college, one is at university, one in an architect's office, another in a book publisher's and one in medical work.

It is a mistake to treat the ex-addict in the early stages of rehabilitation as a normal person. As an addict he was a dying person. When someone arrives at our centre we have constantly to remember that he is extremely disturbed, often far more so than is apparent. Thoughtlessness towards him can be very harmful. Gentle, loving pressure has to be exerted to hold him to the disciplines of the community.

There is no room for the residential Christian counsellor to fall out with his colleague, to show fits of bad temper or aggressiveness or to be distressed or tense about his personal problems. If the Lord is not big enough to deal with these things, how can you tell the residents that God is able to help them? Love is the therapy we must show, ministering it as a healing balm.

However wonderful it may sound to rush off and try to establish a residential rehabilitation centre for addicts, please remember that enthusiasm is not enough in this kind of work. A direct and definite call from God is essential. Anything less is presumption. A call is the authority to do the work we are doing. Good motivation alone is no basis for a God-glorifying work. The person called is first and foremost under God's authority. God's Word is his contract of employment.

8 / The identity crisis

Early in the work of our Rehabilitation Centre, when our experience in the residential care of one-time drug-users was limited, a young boy, who had had a serious drug problem, came into our care. At an early age he had lost his mother and other tragedies had happened around him, making him inward, rebellious and silent. One day he came to me asking to see the doctor because he had boils and spots on his back which were causing him real pain. Most drug-users think naturally of going to the doctor the moment anything goes wrong with them. A pill, or bottle of medicine, is the answer to everything. This tendency must be corrected. However, on this occasion, knowing only a little about such things, I arranged for the doctor to see this lad. The doctor identified the problem as being the boy's need of a good bath and clean underwear. Naturally, the patient refused to accept the doctor's diagnosis and was really very angry indeed, to such an extent that the doctor, a Christian, had to say to me that only the Lord could get the message through. For days afterwards we counselled this young man to see the wisdom of the doctor's advice, to see that he wasn't trying to bring him down or anything like that, but he had simply seen that the need was for more hygiene; that, after all, we had asked him for a 'cure' for boils and he had prescribed a bath!

This boy had bathed only once in six weeks, never wore underwear and had worn the same pair of dirty jeans non-stop to work in, play football in and relax in. We even wondered if he slept in them! (Of course our rules of hygiene today make it impossible for anyone to behave like that, but these were pioneer days.) Finally, I managed to persuade our reluctant bather to try a little bath. Also, one of the staff had a brainwave and took him out and bought him the brightest coloured underpants I'd ever seen! This made him at least willing to try them on. Gradually, the bathing became more attractive to him, until, latterly, he was the sweetest-smelling resident we had, talcum and all! Naturally, the boils went and so did this particular young man's resistance to washing and cleanliness. Soon, new clothes followed and with them a new kind of confidence, as he began to identify with his new self. We had all learned something. It is strange that soap and water worked a greater miracle than I've seen for some time in the changing of a personality.

It is our custom, at our Rehabilitation Centre, to have musical evenings from time to time and, in the past, we would let the boys select their own records. Some would even bring these records into the centre when they came. On one of these musical evenings, we were playing record choices and a particularly 'heavy' piece was selected. The record had hardly started, when two boys jumped up and left the room. Later, I discovered from them the reason why. They had last heard this music when using drugs, one had been fixing heroin and the music simply reminded him of times he wanted to forget. The other had been using LSD heavily and this particular piece of music figured very much in the times he used to use the drug. Listening to it was enough to start his mind working and the 'flash backs', as they are called, started up. This same young man has developed a liking for Handel's music and other classics and is gradually learning to think differently.

It is still a problem for many of these young ex-addicts to live with heavy beat sounds and, if you should ever deal with addicts in your home church, please don't try to win them by taking them to Christian rock music. This sound may be all right for the average youngster who has had no drug or culture problem, but for the one-time drug-user, such music really is dangerous. The musician and composer Jack Ward has said that 'music can lift one to the heights or drag one to the depths and there is often a pandering to the lowest.'

Strange as it may sound, in our centre old-fashioned hymns are loved by our boys; yes, Sankeys and the like. Even Bev Shea and the 'Messiah' are great favourites. I believe that a subtle error has come upon modern-minded Christians today. Many believe that to identify Christ with the modern 'drop-outs' is best achieved by being like them and playing their music. Remember, it is not the words that matter to these young people when they are 'stoned' on drugs, it is just the 'beat'. Christian or otherwise, it matters little, the 'beat' is enough. It is not surprising that such non-Christian productions as 'Jesus Christ Superstar' have rocketed to fame; large percentages of young Christians patronise this kind of show, and the music is heavy rock. It must be understood that the music produces what the addict might term 'vibrations' like certain drugs do. Watch a group of youngsters when this music is being played at full volume. They are often described as being 'sent' or 'turned on'. Until he is really strong, the one-time drug-user should not be exposed to this kind of music on his own.

It really is essential that the person working with the addict realises the very real dangers associated with music and tries to cultivate in his ex-addict friend new appreciation of other music, as he must 'identify' with a new standard.

The single, most significant factor, other than music, that came in with the 'Beat' generation was hair length. As far as one can say, starting with the Beatles, hair styles among young men became longer and longer until, at one point near the peak of the 'hairy' revolution, some males were sporting hair that almost touched the floor and many wore it down to the small of their backs. Jokes by the hundred were told on stage, television and radio about these hairy young people and, at one time, it really was becoming hard for many members of the older generation to tell one sex from the other!

While the liberation which this fashion brought was, in many ways, good, and not a few of the more daring of the older generation allowed their hair to grow longer than they had done previously and were to be seen wearing clothes to business in the City which, at one time, would have assured them of notice of dismissal on the spot, there were and still are serious issues involved in this hairy liberty.

Although hotly disputed, there is no doubt that, for a vast majority of the long-haired youngsters of the day, there is a distinct culture attached to this 'hippy' look which goes with denim jeans and jackets, boots and beads. There is the hippy look; the 'heads' are those who have something that the rest of society seems to lack. This may be true in some ways, but what they 'have' may not necessarily be what we all need. Indeed, associated with the hippy appearance is the drug image, and so often also many other forms of revolutionary thinking and behaviour. If the clothing and hair styles were truly an expression only of individual freedom, they would be acceptable, but, because to the drug-user the clothing, language and hair give him a certain security in these things, they need to be gradually removed in any process of re-habilitation or spiritual cure. In most cases, the very suggestion to a young drug-user that he should cut his hair fills him with fear and rebellion and, in our Centre, such a suggestion causes a major crisis. However, over the years, we have learned that the hair has to go, because before the one-time drug addict can be said to be free from drugs, he must also be free from his culture, and hair and clothing are part of the culture. These things, after all, always reflect the culture of a particular society or nationality. 'Clothing doesn't matter,' the uninformed might argue, yet clothes truly do make a man, as the old saying goes, and a change of clothes and hair styles often marks the first step towards a complete remaking of a life once dominated by drugs and the lowered standards of the hippy society.

We can best describe these issues of clothing, hair, music, etc., as the 'identity crisis'. By this, I mean that moment when the one-time drop-out decides that he no longer wishes to be identified with the past which he once held on to with such tenacity. In a way, it doesn't matter if he still looks the same in appearance but, in order to effect that change of identity, he needs to have an aim, something to give him a reason to be different.

Christians need to beware of the dangers of trying to win the hippy for Christ by identifying with his culture under the misapprehension that to the hippy a 'turned on' Christian will seem more on his wave length. This is completely untrue and, indeed, if a changed life is really to be brought about, the one-time addict needs to be shown that coming to Christ isn't just another drug trip, but a vital and relevant experience, an encounter with God, a move into the miraculous.

There is little doubt that, in the case of the first young boy I mentioned, the victory over bathing was a turning point in his whole experience. It marked a point of changed attitude, a place where he could identify with a new way. Music, clothing and hair styles all reflect a certain way of life. These things might not be bad in themselves, but they have associated ideas in the mind of the one-time drug-user, giving him a false sense of security. One boy frankly admitted to me that he would not tidy his hair up or wear 'straight' clothes when he first came into our rehabilitation centre, because he wasn't sure if he could make it without drugs and the hair and clothes made it possible for him to still think in the old way when he looked in the mirror for assurance, even after his four-week old conversion. 'If I do go back on drugs, this way I won't have so far to go to get back!' was his statement. In other words, in the spirit he was trusting Christ, while, in his mind, he was still relying upon his old image. The very thought of changing this identity filled him with genuine fear.

Now, we have learned that there is no point in laying the law down. The change must come from within, but loving and gentle pressure is often needed. You may find that a boy or girl who comes out of the 'old' culture into your home or church is still not certain of his place. You must gently steer him or her into a relationship with well balanced Christians, who are tolerant, open-hearted, broad-minded and very ordinary. Please don't find the 'way out' members of your church or group to care for him, because they may incur the risk of pushing him back. The boy I have mentioned was fond of using the words of Paul in 2 Corinthians 5:17, 'If any man be in Christ he is a new creature: old things are passed away; behold, all things are become new.' Unfortunately, there was still a great deal of land to be possessed in this young boy's life. The moment must come when the crisis of identity is faced by the one-time drug-user. You, who may deal with him in depth, must be prepared to confront him with this issue. Young people need an ideal to base their lives on. They are, in fact, 'idealists' and this is wonderful. However, the ideal with which they need to identify, when it is in the form of a human being, must have something to offer. Only if we, who try to help these young people, are looking unto Jesus can we ever hope to set a standard that will be strong and satisfactory enough for them to identify with—'be thou an example . . .' The young person knows better than you just how important the matter of identification really is. Let him see that only a true resting in Christ, and abiding in the arms of Jesus, can effect the fullest possible change, leading him out of bondage into life.

Some may think that this subject has been over-simplified. I realise that there is much more that one could say, but that would require a whole book. I should just say, however, that there are many narcotic addicts who never identify with the hippy culture as such, (this, in the main, is an 'acid' or 'speed' scene). But the heroin addict also must face the identity crisis. In his case, it will be shifting his dependence from the doctor and the daily dose of heroin to the Lord Jesus Christ. You will need to keep off the subject of drugs, which, I fear, many sincere, but foolish Christian people find hard to do. Don't be tempted to put him up on a platform to testify at the drop of a hat. His time will come, but care and love will need to be administered. Perhaps the most effective aid of all in dealing with the problem of identity is to establish a real friendship with the one-time drug addict. This is so important for any drug-user. Let him make a real friend of you, if you are a mature and stable Christian. Remember Paul's words: 'We were ready to share with you not only the Gospel of God, but also our own selves . . .' That will be costly, but then you shouldn't even be in touch with such young people if you are not prepared to make some sacrifice.

9 / The addict and ex-addict in the home

One of the greatest needs in the care and after-care
of those addicted to drugs is for Christian families who are prepared to take young people into
their homes and hearts. All Christian bodies working with addicts recognise this need as one of the
most basic factors in long-term help for the drug
user. In our own work, we are able to do a great
deal to help an addict, by leading him to Christ and
training him to take his place in the world again,
but we cannot manufacture a family to which he
can feel he belongs.

More often than not, if a drug addict has been to
a residential centre, it is inadvisable to send him
back to his old environment. This will almost certainly mean that he cannot successfully return
home, at least not for some time, possibly two
years or more. I am constantly telling those who
work in our own ministry of Life for the World
that a spiritual rebirth and 'infilling' of the Holy
Spirit must be accompanied by the discipline of a
growing Christian character. There are no short
cuts to successful living.

The power of God breaks the bondage to drugs
by giving the one-time addict a new peace and joy
and love, but the long-term work of the Holy
Spirit is done through a daily walk with God and
adherence to His Law. Well said are the words of
King David in Psalm 119: 'Wherewithal shall a
young man cleanse his way? By taking heed
thereto according to thy word . . . Thy word have I
hid in mine heart, that I might not sin against thee.'

Gradually, the one-time drug dependant becomes dependent upon the Law of God and on spiritual fellowship with Christ. The things he once saw as 'off beat' and 'establishment' must become part of him, such as holding down a good job and keeping himself clean and having a respect for authority. All this starts to take place when he first becomes a Christian, but, make no mistake about it, until this change has been perfected and can be seen to have taken place, his prognosis is still suspect. In other parts of this book, I have emphasised my own conviction that even hair styles and clothing fashions need to change; this could be extended to music and other forms of entertainment.

I am concerned that, in recent days, well established Christians, who were brought up with 'conservative' convictions, have fallen into the mistaken position of dressing, talking and even thinking like hippy young people, in an attempt to identify with them and help them to become Christians. This is nothing less than compromise and should be resisted, especially in the work of reaching and reclaiming addicts. They are not impressed by pop music Christian-style, or by 'pop Christians'.

By far the most sensible approach for the Christian worker in caring for the addict, is to find a home for him in a Christian family where 'old-fashioned' standards still matter, a family which is not afraid to be thought 'square'. We serve only to hinder his progress if we encourage the addict to think that being a Christian means to be a respectable drop-out. Be warned; if you have witnessed to a young drug-user and seen him or her converted, do not think as long as he or she continues in the hippy culture that you have finished your work; it is only just starting and the 'Jesus trip' can be as empty as the 'acid trip', if it is merely emotional response.

The finest place for the one-time addict to learn new rules for living and gather enough strength to face the tests and trials of his new life is a Christian home. Many reading this book may be asking the question 'What can I do to help the drug addict?' If you have a happy Christian home, then you have a ready-made rehabilitation centre. The Christian home can be the doorway to heaven for many a young man or woman, a training school in love and a proving ground for faith. If you have a spare room and a lot of spare time and love, then you can help a one-time drug addict in many ways. There are just a few basic rules.

1. *Be sure to become committed.*

If you feel that your role is to offer a home for a one-time drug-user, or young person who has been in the culture of the drug-taker, make sure that you are willing to make it a life's work. It might not demand that of you, but be ready. To love anyone enough to change their direction involves a great deal of personal commitment to that redirecting.

I have already talked about getting involved at a deep level and this becomes especially important when you take a young person into your home. Take a good long look, together with the other members of your family, at the home you are will-

71

ing to share. Forget the glamour of taking in an ex-addict. That quickly fades, as do the smiles and assurances of gratitude. Try to see this new member of your family in your home, needing your love and time, expecting it because you will have offered it. It will be too late a week after he arrives to change your mind, and a conditional welcome is worse than no welcome at all.

Often, well-intentioned folk have taken a young person like this into their homes and then discovered too late that it was a mistake and asked him to leave. He feels rejected, hurt and often bitter. You do him greater kindness to let him stay on the street. Try not to let your heart rule you without applying wisdom.

Perhaps your role is simply praying and giving, not taking in the lost and lonely. Many Christians feel that they ought to always open their doors, for the Scriptures teach us to be given to hospitality. However, it is more than hospitality we are talking about; it is adoption, almost. I have seen more tragic results than I care to remember from well-meaning people getting tired of the needy young person they have befriended. Often such youngsters turn up on our doorstep, bitter, resentful and hurt. Therefore, please don't take anyone into your house or family before deciding to commit yourself.

2. *Your home is not a hospital.*

Many folk feel that they are qualified to take an addict literally off the streets and care for him in their homes and try to do the doctor's job for him, or even the Holy Spirit's work. The home is not the right place to withdraw an addict from drugs, or even to let him fix or use drugs in. Leave that to people who are qualified to give expert care. The valuable role of the Christian home is always in the after-care stages.

3 *You must be firm while being kind.*

So many of us who love people and particularly care about youngsters in trouble, tend to be soft and rather naïve when it comes to having these young folk in our homes. Many Christian people allow these youngsters to do things that they would never have let their own children do, or do themselves. They think it is the right course to let them have their own way, even when to allow such freedom means a lowered standard.

I have often wondered how it can be that Evangelical Christians, who have been brought up in a structured home environment, with rules for living and thinking and even dressing, can allow the drop-out youngster to get away with a much lower standard than they allow themselves in hygiene and attitude. If there is washing up to be done, or cleaning, then be sure that the young man you have taken into your home does his fair share. If he has been to a Christian centre prior to coming to you, then he will be used to doing his share. Don't be taken in and fall into the trap of too much kindness. Love is not weak, but strong.

4. *Be prepared for 'failure'.*

Having said something about the necessity of being committed, I must qualify this slightly, in view of the fact that there may be times when a young person comes into your home prematurely, and, through no fault of the family, it may become necessary to ask him to leave. Always remember that you cannot change the life of the one with you, only the Holy Spirit can do this.

5. *You must have a stable home life.*

It would seem only natural to expect that your home is a happy one. Who is the head, for example? Is father really honoured and respected, as well as loved? Is his word important to every other member of the family? Father, do you have the right to a position of honour, not only biblically, but by your example of love and leadership? If you are ever to help one of these young people, your home must be happy and well balanced. This means that mother, no matter how spiritual she may be, must not be the decision-maker in these respects. She should be the quiet, ever-loving confidante and adviser, the home-maker, working as a member of a team with her husband and the rest of the family.

Unless you have a harmonious family atmosphere, you will never see any real work done with the young people you have in your home. It will be like the seed that was sown by the wayside, swiftly snatched away by the 'birds of the air'.

Remember to keep the rules of the household

74

and to teach them to the new member of your family. It has been wrongly said that 'rules are made for breaking'. See to it that, in your home, the rules are kept. Usually, the one-time drug-user who comes to your home will have been taught the vital necessity of learning new and inflexible rules in the training he has had. This is especially so in our own programme of training, where our staff are taught to expect the young people who come into our care to keep all the rules.

Young people, no matter what their background, will test the rules and see just how far they can go. No matter how near or far the fences might be, they will always go to the furthest point. Therefore, be sure to set the boundaries near to home. Yes, they may break your rules, but don't make the mistake of removing them. Youth needs a lead today. Young people are looking for someone to lead them; let your home be a light to them, let them find in it all the guidance they need, as well as all the love. Rules applied with love and justice can become the moulding factor in a young person's life which will make him into a strong and worthwhile citizen.

A further word needs to be said about the difference between spiritual wisdom and kind-heartedness. This may be almost impossible for the 'kind-hearted' Christian to accept, but if you are really to help the addict, or any other young boy or girl to overcome their 'culture' problem and become really free in the long term, then it is essential that you ask the Lord for the wisdom and courage to say 'no' when you do not really feel able to help.

If you are the big-hearted, ever-open-door type of person, then please exercise caution if the one you welcome in is a drug-user. Often work that we have started in the lives of addicts has been short-circuited by a well-meaning Christian friend inviting them to come to their home at any time! They will take up such offers literally. Just thinking that all you need to do is give a young drop-out a home and love is wrong thinking, for he must be given strong leadership and a control in his life, to enable him to live within the new home environment, making new friends, establishing new ideals and standards. If he thinks that you will always take him in, he won't ever try to cope with his problems and will simply 'drop out' from reality by hiding behind your well-intentioned, but misguided love and kindness.

Should an addict come to your home still part of the drug culture, then it is better that you get in touch with one of the voluntary bodies, such as Life for the World, who can best help with advice and residential care.

10 / The addict and ex-addict in the church

If care is needed in the home when you take a drug-user in, then even greater care is needed in the 'spiritual home', the church. In recent years, the established churches have been receiving, broadside on, criticism and attacks on almost every point of faith, practice and doctrine. It seems that, all over the western world, Christian leaders are being forced into a degree of heart searching by the modern-day prophets of doom, represented by all colours and types of 'Jesus People', 'Street People', 'switched-on' parsons and evangelists, who have simply put into new words the old harsh criticism of the established Church. The last decade has been a time of real earth-shattering experience for many well-established Christians, starting possibly with the charismatic movement. This largely provided the impetus for the more recent Jesus revolution and its off-shoots, resulting, in many places, in mass movements of Christians out of well-established churches into 'house churches' and, more recently, the wholesale condemnation of 'organised religion' by the zealous and numerically strong, modern Jesus People.

The church has long been able to stand against such shaking experiences and, if the Lord tarries, will stand it again. Many of these youngsters, and I fear older charismatic Christians also, make the same error of confusing the visible bricks and mortar church with the spiritual and invisible 'body of Christ', to which all true believers in the Lord Jesus Christ belong. Having worked with drug addicts and street people and worshipped with the Jesus people of California, not to mention my own personal charismatic experience, I know that it is wonderfully possible for the ordinary, square, stuffy, 'straight' local church to become a power house and a tremendous source of real blessing to a one-time drug-user or, indeed, any so-called drop-out.

I am often asked by church members how I think 'they' can ever help the young drug-user. The question is asked when they already know the answer, or at least think they know the answer, because most of the Christian periodicals have made the average middle class Christian feel out of touch, out-of-date and too ordinary by far ever to attract the drop-out. A modern Christian poet ends one of his verses with this note of condemnation, given as the reason why ordinary Christian folk don't understand the modern youth culture—'Your religion is middle class'. This 'left wing' thinking among modern Christians is a dangerous trend at the worst and extremely misleading at least. Let me assure you that you don't have to change your dress and hair style or employ a drama-school trained assistant minister. Nor do you need to hold youth rallies with the sound of heavy rock music to bring the youngsters in. I know this sounds old-fashioned, but then the Gospel is, according to the Apostle John, exactly that, ever old, yet ever new! Happening in history, yet relevant today, existing in time, but leading men into eternity. It is out-dated to say this, but just be yourself. As I have pointed out already in an earlier chapter, emotion, real spiritual love is what young people are seeking today, the love of 1 Corinthians 13, full of tenderness and long-suffering, seeking the best, looking for the good in people, forgiving, seeking to build up, not pull down. If you, by the love and power of the Lord Jesus Christ, can genuinely show a youngster that love, simply and without 'side', then you have all you need.

It is a fact today that many older, mature Christians have been led into the mistaken view that if you aren't young any more, you can't reach the young. You must have been a drug addict to understand the addict, you must wear long hair to be accepted by the drop-outs and drug addicts, the old hymns and songs are too out-of-date to be acceptable to youth; this is all untrue. One popular 'Jesus person' claims that he could never get near to the drug takers of the USA dressed in ordinary clothing, as they would think that he was one of the drug squad or an informer. This kind of information has caused many orthodox Christians to form the mistaken impression that they will never be able to reach the addict. Yet I have worked in depth at every location with drug addicts, drop-outs, beatniks and hippies while I had a short hair style and an ordinary style of clothing. In fact, when I started my work in 1964, I used to wear my only good suit to visit the London areas where addicts were, which was my 'Sunday go to meetings suit', clerical grey; I stand 6′ 3″ tall and I wore a long dark blue overcoat! The youngsters I used to go to would joke with me and say that I looked like the 'fuzz', or the drug squad in my clothing, but I assure you that this never affected the Holy Spirit's ministry to these young people and never was a door, however secret, closed to me. The Rev David Wilkerson, who founded one of the most effective teenage drug rescue works, was a 'skinny preacher', to use his own description, and still wears conventional clothes and preaches the simple Gospel to drop-outs, addicts and prostitutes. His is no 'Turn on to Jesus' ministry; it is the square, old, yet ever new Gospel.

It is what is in the heart that matters. If God calls a man, no matter what he wears, he will get through. Indeed, you would need to search your hearts very carefully if you couldn't get through without the trappings in dress and language, for this would be man's work and not the Holy Spirit's. In any case, if the argument was true that you must be like them to reach them, or that you must have been through what they've been through to understand, then one wonders what the male gynaecologist is going to do for his female patients, seeing that he has never had a baby himself!

If you have a message of love to give to young people today, and they know that you love them and understand them no matter what they look like, then they will listen to you, and your home and your church, however 'square', will be the 'in' place for them.

It is so important to underline this fact that, in order to get through to anyone, the Holy Spirit Himself must do the work. If we depend upon gimmicks of any sort, in music, dress or fashion, then the work will be shallow and not God's work at all.

In much of the work done among drug addicts in these days, folk ask why it is that these lives are not changed as they were in the days of William Booth. Where are the mighty, life-transforming experiences of Jesus Christ? they ask. Why do so many of these young people stay in their cultural rut or fall away altogether? The reason can be traced to the shallowness of the evangelism done among them, and this is usually because older and wiser Christians leave the all-important work of witnessing and counselling to young, immature Christians, who have not had sufficient experience of God's grace in their own lives to bring such people right through. Thus a superficial, purely emotional experience takes place and not a real transformation of the Holy Spirit in the life. Mature Christian, there is work for you to do and for your church alongside the young Christian, each of you making your own contribution.

I was led to Christ at the age of fifteen by a man much older than myself, who in so many ways saw things differently from me. He dressed differently, he had a different class background, he was what most people would describe as 'old-fashioned'. Yet all this mattered very little, because my need wasn't for a human answer to my heart's need, but a spiritual answer. I needed Christ and it was He who met me as a young teenager; His grace touched my heart. The person who led me to that place where Christ could reach me was simply introducing me to his friend, Jesus.

The counsellor, or friend, who leads someone to Christ is only an intermediary who provides the introduction; it is the Holy Spirit who does the work. This is true of every real conversion and most Christians are aware of this fact and accept it. However, when we turn to the addict or unattached young person, a different kind of evangelism appears. The old-fashioned, 'ordinary' Christian feels unequal and unable to communicate, thinking that he is too old-fashioned and out of touch with the younger generation. This is so wrong, for it is Christ you are presenting, not yourselves. Remember, this was the whole point of the Apostle Paul's preaching: 'We gave you the Gospel of Christ, not ourselves, not our wisdom, or cleverness, but the Power of God.' Christian friend, you can't save a single soul, only Christ can do this and only the Holy Spirit can draw that seeking soul to Jesus. Do be warned off this popular idea that the so-called 'sleepy' church and ordinary church member will never be able to reach the addict. If you seek to be full of the Holy Spirit, then you will be a channel of real blessing, no matter what your background.

Often, the value of the local church is disregarded in this type of ministry to drug addicts and the like. 'Modern'-thinking evangelists have given the impression that the ordinary church, no matter how evangelical, will never attract the addict into the dry monotony of Sunday worship. However, this idea is what is undermining the ongoing work among such people, who feel that it is not necessary to be a regular worshipper with God's people. The whole concept of worship is never put over to these young people. They are led into the spiritual new birth with the idea that worship must always and only be a time for 'pop' style music, 'turned on' preaching and hand and arm waving. This might have a place, but it is false to imagine that these young people cannot adapt to an ordinary church service. It is essential to teach them that corporate worship of God is part of the Christian experience and that meeting with all classes of the Lord's people is essential. They are often surprised at how alive, straightforward Christians can be, even if they do wear only grey suits! It is also important to show them that worship with people of the same mind is wonderful, but also that the real liberty of the Spirit makes it possible to worship the Lord individually, while meeting with a group of ordinary Christians in a very 'ordinary' church. You will do real harm to the ex-addict who has found Christ if you encourage him to be dissatisfied with the ordinary, straight church fellowship. Show him that great youth services are fine for a time, but meeting regularly with the Lord's people is a privilege and joy—provided that the Lord's people are full of the Lord's love!

Some are placing quite a lot of emphasis upon the concept of an 'addict's church' and I'm not at all sure if I like the principle behind it. The ordinary local church will never become alive to the needs of young people if it is not given the opportunity to respond to them in its midst. In any case, spiritual 'therapy', as such, in the cure and rehabilitation of drug addiction, is a recognition in the final analysis of the simple power of the 'old-fashioned' Gospel. The addict who comes into our centre for rehabilitation is taught to respond to the authority of God's word and the discipline of His people. He is encouraged to see that he is part of a wider family, not just that of the group in which he presently finds himself. Most of the 'Encounter Group' therapeutic centres which have come to Great Britain from America encourage a group loyalty or an almost slavish dependence and those addicts who are helped in these centres find themselves unable to cope alone, away from the group, for any lengthy period. Considering that these are non-religious groups, they are effective in their own way, but definitely maintain the addicts' culture in their centres and afterwards, to assist the long-term cure. Spiritual or Christian healing is based upon dependence upon the Lord and not upon man, or a group of men. However, fellowship, which is fundamental to all men, is basic in the Christian family and, as Christians, we have an abundance of such fellowship all over the world.

The local church is full of caring people, no matter how 'dead' they may seem. I like to think that these young people coming into the church will set it alight again; anyway, most Christian folk look for a challenge and one discovers that churches are as sensitive to spiritual death within their fellowships as their critics. The ex-addict, who has known the rarified atmosphere of being with like-minded people such as exists in our centre, needs to be weaned from such a group and integrated into the more stable and common church family. To suggest to him that anything else might exist with more attraction for him, only causes distress and a wandering spirit and deprives the local church of blessing. He needs to see that all over the country there are groups of the Lord's people, who may be out of touch, but, because they love Jesus too in the same way as he, are open to being made aware of his need. In our work we see the local church as a healing community, made up of unsung therapists and psychologists and counsellors; mums and dads who can make a warm home available; 'mothers in Israel' types, who can warm the heart of any young boy or girl if given the opportunity. There are youth groups, wives' groups and men's groups. The local church is rich in healing resources and to bring a young ex-addict into the fellowship will give the Christians there an opportunity to respond.

In Hong Kong, where one in forty of the population is addicted to drugs, the Chinese churches have tended to be cold towards work with addicts. We are linked to a Chinese Christian work, similar to Life for the World, called Operation Dawn, which is wholly run by Chinese Christians. However, they receive very little support from the churches. When I visited Hong Kong and met church leaders, I discovered that really they were afraid of the addict and didn't know what they could do to help. It wasn't that they didn't care, they just didn't understand. When I addressed pastors of these churches, and talked about the Christian's responsibility, I found a growing concern and love, which only the Lord's people can know.

As I shared with them the work we are doing and the responsibility of the church, there was a new attitude, which has since produced real support for the work of Operation Dawn.

Real conversion of the life-transforming nature

of the New Testament conversion is universal. Drug addicts are no different in this from anyone else. In our centre, some time ago, a young hippy-style addict came for help. He was a rebel in every sense of the word. He hated Christianity and, having been brought up in a Christian home and also attended college until his drug addiction forced him to leave, he knew all the answers! Talking to him on a spiritual level was almost impossible, because he was so arrogant and had erected a wall so high that nothing human could penetrate it. He would respond to the music of his culture, he did wear hippy-style clothing and possibly would have responded to a 'turned on' Christian. However, the turning point in his life came one Easter Sunday, after he had been with us for only a few weeks. His pride and arrogance were foremost right up to the day of his conversion, but it happened so simply, after the morning communion service. I had preached that day of the Christ of Calvary, of the Blood of His Cross, the all-consuming love of a Saviour who forgives over and over again, whose grace is so rich and free. We all felt the Lord present that morning at our simple worship around His table. After the service, as the folk were slowly leaving the chapel, I sat and played some music on the little organ. After a while, I became aware of another noise, which was clearly audible during the quieter passages on the organ. I looked up and there, sitting in the back row of empty chairs, was this young man, his head hung low, his long hair covering his face, and his whole body shaking. My co-Director, John Harris, was the only other person in the room and he was in tears too as he looked across at this young rebel, who was so obviously experiencing an encounter with God. I stopped playing and went over to this young man, now so broken, and put my arm on his shoulder. He murmured that he was arrogant and proud and so sinful; he wept and wept in the presence of the Lord of Calvary. I left him to weep and later we knelt down in the presence of this matchless Christ and he prayed, asking the Lord Jesus to come into his heart and to take away his rebellion and sin, to forgive and cleanse a young lifetime of disobedience to God's holy law. I became so aware, that day, of the power of repentance and confession and the fact that it was all the work of the Holy Spirit and none other. His was a simple, childlike response to the Lord Jesus and he found a peace which has lasted to this day.

I record this story to underline my earlier point that it is the Lord who saves, not man. Churches who fall into the trap of thinking that they are out of touch with these young folk are also in danger of becoming out of touch with the Lord Himself. The local church is the very place to encourage youngsters to go and you, who make up these fellowships, should prepare yourselves to be used. If you feel old-fashioned and out of touch, then that should drive you even more to your knees to seek the Lord's help to communicate your faith. But if you can be yourself, then God will do the rest. Faith should not stand in the wisdom of men, but in the power of God, so said the great Apostle.

This same young man whom I mentioned came with me, some few weeks later, to the church of my good friend, the Rev Francis Dixon, in Bournemouth. He was still long-haired and looked his young nineteen years. However, that church welcomed him so sweetly (that's the only word for it), from the pastor to the congregation, who showed that they cared and were sensitive to his feelings. Although many of the church members were years his senior, this didn't seem to be relevant, for this was the family of God, caring and hoping for one young man. Some months later, I revisited the church and, one after the other, church members came to me asking how my young friend was, telling me that they never ceased to pray for him and I believed them.

Some might have argued that the age group in that church was too mature for this young man, that the services were too conventional, but this is irrelevant if the people are the Lord's, for their very love for Jesus brings Him into every service and where He is, there is fullness of joy! I rejoiced in what I saw at Lansdowne Baptist church, because it was the New Testament in action, young and old members of the church caring and being humble enough to show that concern. If you ever go to that part of the country, make a point of visiting the church and feel that caring, Spirit-filled atmosphere.

There are many churches like this around the country, some small and others bigger like Lansdowne. I believe that the Lord's people long for an opportunity to show their love for young people in need and we, who work with such people, should give the churches the opportunity they desire. If you are a member of a local church which longs for a ministry to youth, then you can start, because you have all the potential. Open your hearts and your church and God will use you.

11 / Utilising the resources of the local church

The local church is rich in therapeutic resources and many doctors recognise just how valuable the church fellowship is in many areas of the healing work among those who are mentally sick. This is no less so with the drug addict, although, in the main, the work of the local church comes into its own in the realm of aftercare, following a period of rehabilitation in a Christian centre. However, often the problem is identifying this potential and using it. In this chapter, I would like to point out, briefly, areas in which your church might usefully become a healing centre for young addicts or ex-addicts, who may come into the church family. Remember, don't let the critics of the local church play down the effectiveness of your role, there is a work for every church fellowship, for the church is the body of Christ and where He is, there is healing in His wings.

The Pastor or Leading Elder

The pastor of any church is the most over-worked member of the fellowship and, as such, is not really the best person to deal with the problems of 'in-depth' counselling which will be required if one is to reach the addict's need or follow-up the ex-addict. Often, long hours of just being with a young person are needed and the pastor cannot give this time, when he has so many other duties in the ministry and leadership of the church.

However, there is a sense in which the pastor must be involved, if only to keep in touch from time to time with the particular problems that only a trained man can deal with, or at least advise on. But don't expect too much of the minister of your church. It is unfair to accuse him of not caring enough for young people like this; he cannot give the time that is needed and you must appreciate this. There are many folk within the church and district with an equal call upon his time and he is also called to a study and ministry of the Word of God. Therefore, the pastor must be seen as the head of the therapeutic team, but others must be involved in the work.

The Ministry of Hospitality

In every church family, there are those who have a special gift for hospitality. It would be wise to identify these folk and challenge them with the need of the young boy or girl who comes as a stranger into the fellowship. Often, there will be a young couple in the church who feel that they should be using their home more for the Lord, or an older couple who find that their children have grown up and left the family home. These are the people to encourage into a more involved ministry with the addict or ex-addict. I have already said something about using the home for the addict in need of treatment or care, but there is a place for homes for young people who have no real home of their own and who have come from some treatment centre, such as the Life for the World Rehabilitation Centre. It may be that your church would care to consider opening a whole house for the purpose of after-care, with a married couple acting as house parents. The value of this would be that a stable home could be provided, with a local church to be involved in, and with work also near at hand if your church is in an industrial area or a place where jobs are not hard to find.

If this sounds too ambitious for you, then one way to start is to invite a young couple, or any couple for that matter, to make their home available as a contact point to which the young person who has recently joined the church can go. Try to make them aware that they are acting as therapeutic helpers and that what they start they must be in a position to complete.

Visiting

It is vitally important that regular visiting is carried out. If there is no church house, or if the young boy or girl in your church is living at home, then assign a member in the church to visit at least once a week. Don't take it for granted that he or she will come uninvited.

The Church Room

A number of churches have youth fellowship rooms or club meeting rooms, but make a special room for counselling, where there is a bottomless coffee pot and a member of the fellowship always on duty, say three nights a week, for young people to come and meet and talk. There is special value in this if your church is near to a city centre. Many make the mistake of thinking that they must provide a so-called 'Christian coffee bar' to reach such young people. The kind of youngster who is using drugs will not need a place with loud 'pop' music going, just a place to come and meet people who care, that's all. I'm talking generally here, of course, about work with those who have been addicted or are still using drugs.

Parents' Ministry

Find the folk in your church, preferably older people who have children of their own, who would be willing to make a special ministry of visiting the parents of the young people who may come into the church. Often, parents of a drug addict feel guilt-ridden and broken and don't find it easy to communicate their need. It is so wonderful to find others who will talk to them and help them with their own problems, while seeking to solve the problem of their relationship with their children.

Information Service

It would be very helpful if a church was to appoint a member or group of members with a secretary, who would take responsibility for this specialised ministry, so that folk will know who to come to with needs and information. The Probation Service would be pleased to have a visit from such a group, or person, and would offer helpful ways of co-operating. Also, there are many hospitals and doctors who help addicts (see details in the back of this book) and manuals available of workers who can help specifically with drug problems. Christian organisations also exist and one member of the church should have all these details to hand.

Above all, make full use of the membership of the church; involve everyone in this Christ-centred ministry. Show what love really means to these young people, who will come very anxious to be loved.

12 / One step at a time—a summing up

All the energy and faith expended in bringing an addict to the point of abandoning his drugs take us only to the beginning of the real work of the Christian. The really worth-while aim is not just to get an addict to give up drugs, but to lead him into a thrilling experience of God's salvation that will completely obliterate the old life and the old desire for drugs. Our aim is to give stability and purpose to someone who for most of his life has relied on a very corrosive chemical crutch.

As I have said, doctors are surprisingly ready to accept a spiritual answer to drug abuse when they realise that addiction is not responding to medical treatment. In the final analysis we must realise with the Apostle Paul that the only answer lies in Christ and Him crucified. We should not compromise this or we rob the Gospel of its power. The Gospel is the power of God unto salvation, and the only power that will set the drug addict truly free. It cannot be done by the power of psychiatry, psychology or sociology, no matter how well-intentioned. The power of God is sufficient. If you fully believe this then you have in your possession something dynamic to offer.

One day I was faced with a young addict of eighteen who had attempted suicide more than twenty times. I was interviewing him for a place as a resident in our rehabilitation centre. I had never met such a sad-faced and lifeless young man. The experts were abandoning him as someone who would never live without drugs and would not in any case reach the age of twenty-one. The reports described him as a hopeless case, completely incapable of establishing a meaningful relationship with anyone. His probation officer had asked me to have him at my centre because he thought it might add a couple of years to his life.

As I talked to this young addict, he stared at the carpet, stirring only occasionally. His eyes were half-shut and dead. He looked void of life. His arms were scarred in many places from needles and attempts at suicide.

I felt a real love for this sad young man and I knew that it was love that he needed most of all. I told him that God loved him. I told him that He looked on him with great love and saw him as an individual, a person who mattered. I told him that we wanted to show him this in our centre. The simplicity of my approach touched him and he stayed. Only a short time afterwards he found Christ as Saviour. His life was a new adventure, and the shadows of a premature death disappeared. Christ's life began to shine in him and wonderfully change him. He began to laugh, to rejoice in the Lord, to pray, to talk in a lively way. It was just as if someone had got inside this young but darkened man and found the main switch. He lit up and began to live.

The real work in his life was not done when he came off drugs, but afterwards, when he found Christ and began to put his life in step with God. He rejected his hippy way of life and all that went with it. The real work is always in the breaking down of barriers. Addicts erect many barriers around themselves as a protection against the hurt of the world and the hurt that their own foolishness brings.

Old associations and friends prove one of the biggest barriers to overcome. The addicts' subculture is a very involved subject, but briefly it can be said that normal society is abnormal to the addict, He sees the world through eyes clouded by the drugs he consumes. The drugs affect not only his body and brain but his entire way of life. So many parents complain of losing their child when he takes drugs because drugs take over the personality. The addict finds it impossible to relate to ordinary people, often not realising his alienation. He feels one only with other drug-users. This in itself provides a strong incentive for the mild drug-user to leave the 'normal' world behind and go on to using harder drugs.

Another barrier is that of the addict's negative mental attitude, often contrasting strangely with his optimism that he can solve his own problem. The negative attitude is manifested in fits of bad temper, in moodiness and hyper-criticism directed at the one trying to help.

There are other problems also which are directly the concern of the residential worker. One of these is the ex-addict's strong fear of going back into the world, linked with an unwillingness to share problems. The addict is always his own worst critic. He is always dreading relapse. But even at points of crisis he will do his best to conceal these fears. Sometimes, merely to accommodate whoever is helping him, he will manufacture a superficial problem to draw attention away from the real trouble.

Another barrier is that of guilt. Even in long-term care and rehabilitation, often after a year of intensive spiritual therapy, guilt may fill the heart of the former addict. He will be filled with the guilt for his past, especially for sexual sins. He will often feel guilty about hurting loved ones and be possessed by an over-riding sense of unworthiness. This can be overcome only by patience, love and prayer. Only Jesus can give the guilty conscience peace. As Christians we have the perfect remedy for guilt—'The blood of Jesus Christ cleanses us from all unrighteousness'.

I have tried in this book to present two aspects of the Christian's role in the evangelism and care of those addicted to drugs—the fundamental need for a clear and uncompromising presentation of Jesus Christ as the only hope for real and lasting restoration of the drug-user; and a Holy Spirit wisdom to co-operate with those who care for drug dependents professionally, thus maintaining a consistently balanced Christian witness. It would be helpful therefore, if to sum up these points, I was to outline a step by step guide for those who may encounter an addict in need both spiritually and socially.

1. When you first come into contact with anyone who you suspect may be using drugs, take great care, remember that you are possibly coming into contact with someone who is incurably ill and very likely, incurably anti-social.

2. Find out all that you can about the drug-user. Don't make him think that you are going

to use any of the information he might give you against him, but ensure that he can see you really care for him as a person—that is important.

3. If the user should come into a meeting or youth club by chance and seem to be very sick, then take him by car to the casualty department of your local hospital. Some drug-users take overdoses by accident and if the one you should encounter is uncontrollably sleepy and shows signs of entering into unconsciousness, then try to find out from him what drugs he last used; this will be essential information for the doctor, then the information in Appendix 2 of this book will apply. REMEMBER, act fast. If someone really has taken an overdose, you cannot hope to do anything spiritually under these circumstances. Remember also, that miracles are sometimes seen in such cases but belong to the sovereignty of God; don't let presumption be a substitute for faith.

4. Remember that your responsibility is to communicate the Gospel message of God's love, that is your role. You may not see the addict delivered there and then from addiction, but you can sow seeds of life and hope into his heart. Make it your business to find out the addresses of organisations and others who can help the drug-user (see Appendix 6).

5. If your contact needs to enter hospital, keep up the friendship and visit regularly with the permission of the doctor. If this drug-user is on probation, let the probation officer know of your interest; he will be very grateful for sane, sensible help from volunteers. NOTE: As a gen-

eral rule, it is best for men to deal with men and women to counsel girl drug-users. There may be exceptions, but it is a rule worth keeping to, for the sake of the one you are trying to help.

6. Write to one of the Christian centres with facilities for caring for your friend on a long-term basis by rehabilitation. Keep them informed; they may ask you to tell your friend about the help they can offer and guide him to contact them, or send someone to meet him. It is essential that you work in co-operation with those most qualified to help.

7. By far the most telling witness of the love of Christ to the drug-user, will be your patient and consistent interest in him. Don't give up, because eventually he will want to know the same Jesus.

8. If he has a family, ask him about them, and see if he minds your visiting them. You may be able to do a great deal of good for parents of addicts by sharing their problems and letting them know that you want to help. Please don't just 'preach' to the addict, stuff a tract in his hand and hope for the best. Follow through, by prayer and concerned action. Never act alone, but share with your minister, elder or older friend. Someone's life is at stake; make your contribution to the whole, God will do the rest.

Finally, seek to counsel and help in the true spirit of Christian love, following that perfect definition sent down in 1 Corinthians 13:

'Love is very patient and kind, never jealous or

envious, never boastful or proud, never haughty or selfish or rude. Love does not demand its own way. It is not irritable or touchy. It does not hold grudges and will hardly even notice when others do it wrong.' *(Living Bible)*.

Let the addict be reached by the strong and wonderful love of God revealed in Jesus through a life dedicated to Him. Let your life be such an example. Love can unlock any door and melt the hardest heart.

Acknowledgements

Appendix 1, 'Drugs and the law' was contributed by Mr Graham Jeffs, Ll.B.

Appendix 2, 'Relevant first aid' and Appendix 4, 'Drugs which are abused' were contributed by Dr George Birdwood.

Appendix 1 / Drugs and the law

The aim of the legislation covering drug abuse is to control the misuse of drugs without making the inevitable black market too profitable and without forcing users to resort to criminal activities to obtain a supply.

The Dangerous Drugs Act of 1967 was the first real attempt by Parliament to attack drug abuse. The regular supplier of heroin, that is the National Health Service, was all but eliminated. General Practitioners lost their power to prescribe heroin and cocaine. The price of heroin immediately rocketed as addicts were forced to attend clinics to obtain a supply. But it was not long before the vacuum in the market was filled by supplies of illegally imported 'Chinese' heroin. Chinese heroin generally contains only about 35 per cent heroin. The residue consists of caffeine, quinine, strychnine and even rat poison. In buying Chinese the addict has to be involved to some extent in the kind of criminal activities, such as theft and mugging, with which his American counterpart is all too familiar.

Although the mere possession of a controlled drug is usually illegal, regulations made subsequent to the Misuse of Drugs Act 1971 permit those in receipt of a prescription, from a clinic in the case of some drugs or from a General Practitioner in the case of others, to possess those drugs legally.

Not only is unlawful possession an offence, but so too are unlawful supply, production and attempting to procure, and so there are associated offences such as loitering, obstruction and begging. Under the Dangerous Drugs Act 1967, the police have special power to stop and search suspected drug offenders without having to comply with the normal formalities of an arrest.

The Home Office issued in 1972 a directive to police forces that such things as long hair and beads should no longer be the sole grounds for suspicion in order to justify use of the stop-search provisions. However, having searched someone and having found a substance which he suspects may be a controlled drug, a police officer may tell him to appear at a police station at a particular time two or three weeks hence for the result of analysis by the police forensic laboratory.

If the analysed drug is found to be a controlled drug the suspect will be charged and will appear at the local magistrates' court the following morning. If when the search is made the officer is sure of the identity of the drug and/or there is a substantial amount involved, the suspect may be detained at the police station in order to appear in court the next morning.

If you have befriended an addict who gets arrested, remember that he will need your continuing support. He is likely to be confused and frightened. After a poor night's sleep and probably the onset of withdrawal symptoms, he will not really be able to understand all that is going on around him. A police cell is a lonely place. True, he has flouted the law which you yourself respect, but to abandon him now would be to cancel out your witness to him.

When you learn that an addict you know is in custody, telephone the police station and ask the officer dealing with the case what the charges are, and if bail has been granted by the police. If you can visit the station, ask if bail can be granted on recognisance of either the addict or yourself. No money actually changes hands; what it means is that either the defendant or you as his surety state ownership of goods or cash to a certain value which could be realised in the event of the defendant's failure to attend court at the fixed time. Unless you are satisfied as to your friend's reliability, you should not become a surety however disastrous a remand in custody may appear to be for a particular addict. Even if bail is refused at the police station it is possible that the court will grant bail the following day.

Unless the charge is a very minor one, very straightforward, and your addict friend intends to plead guilty, he should be legally represented, which in the vast majority of cases means applying for legal aid. By simply asking for legal aid when he appears in court the following morning (or on Monday if the arrest is on a Saturday), he is also automatically asking the court for an adjournment.

To be legally represented at the first hearing is expensive as there will have been no opportunity to apply for legal aid. But if you think it would be wise to apply for bail at this court hearing, then you should contact a firm of solicitors whose offices are near the courts and arrange for a legal representative to attend. If you are unhappy about the circumstances of the arrest and you are unable to obtain satisfactory answers from the police, you should again arrange for a solicitor to contact or visit the station.

So, at the first hearing the two important things are bail and legal aid, over both of which the court has discretionary powers. The police may object to bail on the grounds that your friend is likely to abscond or because of the serious nature of the case, but the decision is made by the magistrates. Legal aid will be granted by some benches much more easily than by others, but even though the first application is unsuccessful further applications can be made at subsequent hearings. You can help your friend by advising on these matters, and by giving him assistance in completing his legal aid form, especially with the accompanying statement of means. If you know of a sympathetic solicitor you can approach him, but otherwise the clerk's department of the court will supply you with a list of local firms who undertake legal aid work.

If after the first hearing your friend is in custody, you will be able to visit him in the court cells after the court has risen, usually at 1 p.m., and then every day at the remand centre or prison without needing a visiting order. If legal aid has still not been applied for, a form should be obtained from a prison officer and posted when completed to the clerk's department of the appropriate court.

Under the 1971 Act, controlled drugs have been divided into groups A, B and C according to relative harmfulness. The maximum sentences for offences involving A, B or C grouped drugs are seven, five and two years respectively. Maximum sentences for supplying or selling controlled drugs are more severe—14, 14 and five years for the three groups respectively. In practice, the actual sentences imposed vary—conditional discharge, fine, probation, suspended sentence or a custodial sentence—depending on the quantities involved and the defendant's previous convictions.

You will be able to visit an addict in prison once every 28 days for 30 minutes (or more in prisons outside London) providing he sends you the necessary visiting order. In addition, a limited number of letters can be both sent and received. In prison the addict is normally given physeptone tablets on a daily reducing basis for a period related to his dependency when sentenced.

We have noted that the 1971 Act distinguishes between a person who is found in possession of a drug and one who is actively selling or producing drugs, the sentiment being that it is the 'pusher' who should be hit the hardest. Unfortunately the distinction is not all that clearly defined. Often an addict acts as a selling agent and is paid in drugs, and this kind of involvement with others may well mean a more complex charge.

Never forget that when you are working with addicts you are dealing with those in constant danger of breaking the law. Here there are two points worth stressing.

Firstly, there have been convictions of people who have allowed their premises to be used for smoking cannabis. Since 1971 it has been necessary for police to prove that the owner of the property knew that the smoking was going on. But in spite of this safeguard, churches who run coffee bars should be very careful that cannabis is not smoked and that no drugs of any kind are bought or sold on the premises, otherwise they fall under the same kind of penalties as do those who sell drugs to others.

Secondly, you may be faced with a situation in which a user, for one reason or another, hands drugs to you. Under the new law, if you have taken all such steps as are reasonably open to you to destroy the drug or to hand it over to an authorised person, then this will be a defence. But, whatever your motives in the first instance, remember that you could be committing an offence.

Appendix 2 / Relevant first aid

The First Aid for treating an addict who has fallen into a coma following an overdose of drugs is essentially the same as that for treating any person who is unconscious due to sudden illness, to attempted suicide, or even to a simple fainting attack.

The first thing to remember is not to panic. Don't try to rouse the patient by throwing cold water over him. Don't move him at all unless it is for his own safety—for example, if he has fallen near a fire.

Turn the patient face downward, without a pillow, with the head turned to one side. This stops choking due to vomiting and prevents the tongue from falling back into the throat. On no account should a patient be propped up in a chair or allowed to lie on his back.

Remove any false teeth, see that the mouth and throat are clear, and then hold the chin, closing the mouth to prevent choking and so assist breathing. Loosen the collar or any other tight clothing which you think might be restricting breathing.

Telephone 999 and ask for an ambulance. Explain that you have an unconscious patient who appears to be suffering from an overdose of drugs.

Check that the patient's breathing is still clear. If necessary keep him warm with a blanket, but do not use hot-water-bottles.

If the patient can be left, search for tablets, bottles, pill boxes or anything else which would help the hospital to identify the drugs that have been taken. Take them to the hospital together with any vomited material.

When the ambulance arrives ensure that the patient is put on the stretcher in the same semi-prone position.

Never try to get a sleepy or unconscious patient to drink, nor attempt to make him sick. If the patient is still fully conscious after taking an over-dose by mouth, make him sick by pushing a spoon handle or finger down his throat. Then give him a drink of strong, warm, salted water and make him sick again.

Appendix 3 / Addicts' slang

Acid—LSD
Acid-head—LSD-taker

Bag—US term for dose of heroin
Bang—injection or its effect
Bennies—Benzedrine tablets (amphetamine)
Big D—LSD
Black bomber—Durophet (amphetamine)
Black and white (minstrel)—Durophet (amphetamine)
Blocked—under influence of drug, usually amphetamine
Blow—to smoke cannabis
Blues—Edrisal, Drinamyl or other blue amphetamine tablets
Brought down—depressed 'hangover' after-effect of drugs
Buzz—effect of a drug

C—cocaine
Candy—barbiturates
Caps—capsules
Charge—marijuana
Coke—cocaine
Cokie—cocaine-taker
Cold turkey—untreated withdrawal of heroin
Come down—to stop taking drugs
Cook up—to prepare an injection, usually of heroin
Cut—to adulterate drugs with sugar, etc

Dex—dexedrine tablets (amphetamine)

Dixies (Dexies)—dexedrine tablets (amphetamines)

Dominoes—black and white capsules of Durophet (amphetamine)

Drying out—stopping or reducing dose of heroin

Experience—LSD trip

Fix—injection, usually of heroin and/or cocaine

Flash—initial effect of stimulant, cocaine or amphetamine

French blue—Drinimyl or other blue amphetamine tablet

Gear—addict's syringe, etc

Goofballs—US term for barbiturates

Grass—cannabis, usually marijuana

H—heroin

H and C—heroine and cocaine

Habit—dependence on a drug

Happening—effect of marijuana or LSD, also group use

Hash—cannabis, usually resin

High—effect of drugs

Hooked—addicted, usually to heroin

Horse—heroin

Joint—reefer (cannabis cigarette)

Jolly beans—amphetamine tablets

Joy pop—to inject heroin or morphine under skin before addiction develops

Junk—heroin (morphine, cocaine or other drugs)

Junkie—heroin addict

Kick—effect of stimulant, cocaine or amphetamine

Kick habit—to stop taking drugs

Mainline—to inject drugs directly into a vein (usually heroin, morphine, cocaine or methyl amphetamine)

Meth—methedrine tablets or injection (methyl amphetamine)

Minstrel—black and white Durophet capsules (amphetamine)

Needle—addict's syringe

Nod—to doze off after dose of drugs

Pad—room, flat

Pillhead—tablet-taker, usually amphetamines

Pot—cannabis

Pot-head—cannabis smoker

Psychedelic experience—effect of LSD or other hallucinogen

Purple heart—Drinamyl (old shape)

Pusher—drug pedlar

Resin—cannabis resin, hashish, etc

Rope—cannabis

Scrip (script)—prescription for habit-forming drugs

Shoot-up—to inject drugs, usually mainlining

Shot—injection of drugs
Sick—withdrawal symptoms, usually from heroin
Skin popping—injection under the skin, usually heroin
Sleepers—barbiturates
Speed—amphetamines
Speedball—combined injection of heroin (or morphine) with cocaine (or methyl amphetamine)
Spike—addict's syringe, etc
Stick—marijuana cigarette or reefer
Sugar—LSD

Tea—marijuana
Trip—effect of LSD or other hallucinogen
Turn on—to start another person on drugs
Turned on—to be under the influence of drugs

Weed—cannabis, usually marijuana
Works—addict's syringe, etc.

Appendix 4 / Drugs which are abused

Trade names and brief descriptions of commonly used drugs which could be abused.

1. *Some stimulants, etc., controlled by the Drug (Prevention of Misuse) Act 1964*

Amphetamine: plain white tablets, roughly aspirin-sized.

Apisate: largish yellow tablet, W in shield on one side.

Dexamphetamine: plain tablet, white or yellow, sometimes with line on one side.

Dexedrine: flat, yellow tablets with line on one side and SKF on other.

Dexedrine (long-acting): two sizes of capsules, brown one end, transparent the other, containing orange and white granules like 'hundreds and thousands'.

Dexten: large, flat, yellow tablet with cross on one side marked N and 'dexten' on the other.

Duromine: small size, capsule, green one end, grey other, marked Riker; larger size, maroon and grey capsule marked Riker.

Durophet: small size, white capsule marked Riker; medium size, white and black capsule marked Riker; large size, black capsule marked Riker—'black bombers'.

Euvitol: yellow tablets or green liquid.

Filon: orange-yellow, sugar-coated tablet.

Lucophen SA: largish white tablets.

Mephine: ampoules of solution.

Mephentermine: plain tablets.

Methedrine: plain white tablets with line on one side, 'tabloid brand' on reverse.

Methylamphetamine: plain white tablets, or glass ampoules containing colourless solution.

Neo-endrine: nasal spray in plastic bottle.

Parnate: red, sugar-coated tablets marked SKF.

Preludin: flat, white tablets marked P on one side and with a line on the other.

Preludin (long-acting): large, yellow tablets with 'castle' design on one side.

Ritalin: white tablets marked CIBA on one side, line with two dots on other, also ampoules of solution.

Tenuate: plain white tablet, resembling large aspirin.

Tenuate Dospan (long-acting): white bolster-shaped tablet with line across middle.

Villescon: orange, sugar-coated tablet marked with 'castle' design, or orange liquid.

2. *Some mixed stimulants and other drugs controlled by the Drugs (Prevention of Misuse) Act 1964*

Anxine: white sugar-coated tablets.

Appetrol: pink tablets.

Appetrol SR (long-acting): pink-topped capsules.

Barbidex: large, flat tablet, cross on one side, marked N and 'barbidex' on other.

Daprisal: yellow, pillow-shaped tablet marked SKF on one side.

Dexdale: green tablets, line on one side, DPL on other.

Dexytal: bright pink capsules.

Drinymyl: pale mauve-blue tablets with line on one side—'purple hearts'.

Drinymyl Spansules (long-acting): capsules, green one end, transparent other, filled with green and white granules, two sizes.

Durophet M: small size, green and brown capsules; large size, red and brown capsules.

Edrisal: plain blue tablets marked SKF on one side.

Parstelin: green, sugar-coated tablets marked SKF, also as a liquid.

Potensan: maroon, sugar-coated tablet.

Potensan forte: gold-coated pill.

Steladex: capsule, transparent and yellow, filled with blue and white granules.

Stimplete: orange-coloured liquid.

3. *Some commonly used barbiturate preparations*

Amytal: small, plain white tablets.

Carbrital: white capsule with blue line around middle.

Nembutal: bright yellow capsules.

Phenobarbitone: small, plain white tablets.

Phenobarbitone (long-acting): capsules, blue one end, transparent other, containing blue and white granules.

Seconal: orange-red capsules.

Sodium amytal: bright blue capsules.

Soneryl: pink tablets with line on one side.

Tuinal: capsules, orange-red one end, blue other.

4. Some commonly used tranquillisers and non-barbiturate sleeping drugs

Doriden: plain white tablet marked CIBA.

Equanil: tablets in two sizes—yellow and white.

Largactil: white, sugar-coated tablets, syrup or injection ampoules (used to terminate 'bad' LSD trips).

Librium: small size, green and yellow capsules; large size, green and black capsules (also as glass ampoules containing powder).

Mandrax: capsules, dark blue one end, light blue other, marked Mx RL, or in tablet form, flat, white, marked Mx on one side, RL on other.

Miltown: large size, white tablets with line across; small size, white, sugar-coated tablets.

Miltown SR (long-acting): blue-topped capsules.

Mogadon: white tablet, 'Roche' on one side with semicircles, line on reverse.

Oblivon: capsules, or as blue liquid.

Oblivon C: oval, blue, sugar-coated tablets.

Sparine: three strengths—yellow, orange and red sugar-coated tablets, also injection ampoules and syrup.

Stelazine: blue tablets, sugar-coated, marked SKF (two sizes); also in ampoules or in clear, greeny-yellow syrup.

Stelazine (long-acting): capsules, blue one end, yellow the other (three sizes).

Valium: white, yellow or blue tablets (three sizes), also as capsules, syrup and injection solution in ampoules.

Appendix 5 / Questions and answers

1. A minister asks: 'Some young people in my church are keen on helping drug addicts, but there aren't any that we know of in our part of town. They want to go to the West End of London to find young people in need. Is this the best thing to do?'

'Most keen young people feel the desire to go to the more obvious places to find those in need, like Soho in London. But today there is not one area of England where addicts or users cannot be found. It is doubtful whether help in any depth can be given on the streets of any large town. I think it is better for your youngsters to concentrate on youth evangelism in their own area. Drug-users will soon be contacted. It is a mistake for churches to initiate ministry in areas away from the local church as they cannot, in all honesty, give long-term care to addicts from a distance.'

2. 'If a young drug-user came into our church, how could we help?'

'If you are asked for help, there is a great deal you can do. But be sure that if a drug-user comes into your church he really wants to be helped. He may be just curious. Don't ruin an initial contact by being over zealous in preaching the Gospel. Find out as much as you can about him and be friendly. Let him know you are there if he needs you. He will come again if you are attractive Christians!'

3. 'We have a young man who comes into our church who is using drugs. Should we give him money when he asks?'

'It depends what he wants the money for. If you feel a responsibility towards him and he genuinely wants the money for a room or food it is better to pay the rent to the landlord for him and buy him a meal. Better still, see if there is a family in the church who are prepared to offer him a temporary home?

4. 'Where would I start to get involved in the drug problem?'

'Bearing in mind what I have already said about reaching addicts in towns, you could contact your local probation officer and say that you want to help. Or you could contact one of the hospital treatment centres listed at the back of this book and tell them that you would like to be a voluntary worker.'

5. 'Is it necessary for an ex-addict to receive an experience of "speaking in tongues" to keep off drugs?'

'The only way an addict can keep off drugs is to change his direction by a spiritual rebirth. I believe this needs to be a dynamic rebirth. Many young people subsequent to their conversion enter into what is known as a Pentecostal experience. In many cases this is a real and blessed encounter with the Holy Spirit. However, in my experience, it is not a guarantee against temptation or even relapse. Many of the young men in our care have had

120

a deep spiritual experience since their conversion. Some have had a Pentecostal experience and spoken in tongues. Some are working and living in the world today free of drugs. I believe that the real necessity for an addict, as for all men, is regeneration and a life of walking in the Spirit. There is a need to be "filled with the Spirit" as in any Christian's life. I am afraid that there are no short cuts to complete freedom, or instant miracles. These miracles take time. God may well give a spiritual blessing, He usually does, but it is the cross that breaks the chains and the empty tomb that gives the victory.'

6. 'I have a young man in my church who feels a "call" to work with drug addicts. I believe this is a genuine sense of calling, but wonder, as he has no more than three O-level GCE passes. What other qualifications would you recommend and how would you start?'

'A great many young people today, thankfully, are concerned about the spiritual condition of their generation and many are feeling such a call to work with drug addicts. The necessary qualifications depend on what area this young man wishes to work in. The areas of work can be broadly defined in three sections—direct spiritual and social ministry to addicts in a residential setting, church-related voluntary work such as coffee bar and street evangelism, and practical and administrative work in a residential setting.

'I will deal with the last two areas first. To work locally with young people using drugs the main qualification is being definitely in God's will. This kind of work is best carried out with ministers and youth leaders. And as for administrative work, there are many young and middle-aged folk who have a compassion for young addicts in need, but who lack the spiritual maturity necessary for therapeutic work. There are many openings in organisations for those willing to work in gardens and doing general maintenance work such as painting and repairing, cooking and other domestic work. It is an area in which real work can be done for the Lord. And it is an area in which it is not always full-time workers that are needed.

'But the person who wants to commit himself to working in a full-time social and spiritual ministry to young addicts must be aware of a real spiritual authority in his calling, a real, deep sense of God's calling. The desire to help is not enough. The work of residential counselling is certainly as demanding, if not more, than missionary work—so a minister or church should apply the same test to this call as to a candidate for the ministry or missionary service.

'Ideally this person should be over 25 and have some Bible College course. He will need to have worked in his church for some time with young people and it would be helpful if he had contacts with professional social workers, probation officers and others. Although the work he will do will be mainly on the spiritual level, it would be useful if he had the ability to take a university course in social science or some allied subject.

'Above all, he will need sound common-sense, and an ability to stick at the job no matter what. He needs an understanding of people and a loving, patient spirit. He will also be someone who can take and give discipline. It seems hardly necessary to add that he will be a lover of the Word of God and given to prayer.

'Young women who feel similarly called will find it helpful to have experience in social work and youth work. The same spiritual and personal qualities are required. It is often useful to have taken a course in psychiatric nursing.'

7. 'If our church wanted really to help in some practical way, apart from finance, what would you suggest?' asks a minister.

'In the first place, educate your members to take an active interest in anyone in need who comes to the church. Indifference or lack of real concern can turn many away. Then perhaps you could find some families in the church who would be prepared to open their homes on a long-term basis to ex-addicts who have finished a period of rehabilitation.

'Another more definite way in which a church can help is to find those in the church keen to do something constructive for addicts and set up a day counselling centre or evening clinic. You could make it known to the professional bodies in your area that you are prepared to accept people referred to you for Christian counselling. But it is important to work close with existing organisations such as Life for the World and to make sure that your workers receive some sort of training to help them to counsel addicts.'

Appendix 6 / Useful addresses

ASSOCIATIONS, ETC

Association for the Prevention of Addiction, 15 King Street, London WC2 (01-836-3781)

Department of Health and Social Security, Alexander Fleming House, Elephant and Castle, London SE1 (01-407-5522)

Home Office Drugs Branch, Romney House, Marsham Street, London SW1 (01-799-3488)

National Association for the Care and Re-settlement of Offenders, 125 Kennington Park Road, London SE11 (01-735-1151)

Institute for the Study of Drug Dependence, Chandos House, 2 Queen Anne Street, London W1 (01-580-2518)

Institute of Psychiatry Addiction Research Unit, 101 Denmark Hill, London SE5 (01-703-5411)

National Addiction and Research Institute, 533a King's Road, SW10 (Dr Peter Chapple) (01-352-1590)

HOSPITALS GIVING OUT-PATIENT TREATMENT ONLY (London area)

National Temperance Hospital, Drug Dependence Clinic of UCH, 122 Hampstead Road, NW1 2LT (387-5206)

St Giles' Centre, Camberwell Church Street, SE5 (703-5841)

Lambeth Hospital, Brook Drive, Kennington, SE11 (735-8141)

Westminster Hospital Treatment Centre, 48 Vincent Square, SW1 (834-1537)

Queen Mary's Hospital, Roehampton Lane, SW15 (788-7211)

St Mary's Hospital, Harrow Road, W9 (286-4884)

Charing Cross Hospital, Agar Street, West Strand, WC2 (836-7788)

HOSPITALS GIVING IN-PATIENT AND OUT-PATIENT TREATMENT (London area)

St Clement's Hospital, 2a Bow Street, E3 (980-4899)

Hackney Hospital, Homerton High Street, E9 (985-5555)

Simmon's House, St Luke's Hospital, Woodside Avenue, N10 (Adolescents only) (888-8311)

Maudsley and Bethlem Royal Hospitals, Addiction Clinical Research and Treatment Unit, Denmark Hill, SE5 (703-6333)

St George's Hospital, Tooting Grove, SW17 (672-1255)

Tooting Bec Hospital, Tooting Bec Road, SW17 (In-patients only) (672-6655)

LIFE FOR THE WORLD TRUST

Rehabilitation Centre and Administrative Offices: Northwick Park, Blockley, Moreton-in-Marsh, Glos. GL56 9RG (0386-76-440)

London Centre: P.O. Box 100, London E7 ONB (01-534 1861)

Founder/Director: Rev. Frank Wilson

Recommended reading list

Alan Bestic, *Turn Me On Man*. Tandem 1966.

Isador Chein *et alia*, *Narcotics, Delinquency and Social Policy: The Road to H*. Tavistock, 1964.

P. H. Connell, *Amphetamine Psychosis*. Chapman and Hall, 1958.

M. M. Glatt *et alia*, *The Drug Scene in Britain*. Edward Arnold, 1967.

Ernest Harms (Ed), *Drug Addiction in Youth*. Pergamon, 1964.

Paul Hunter and M. J. Delaney, *Needle of Death*. Studio Vista, 1967.

Jeremy Larner and Ralph Tefferteller, *The Addict In The Street*. Penguin, 1966.

Peter Laurie, *Drugs*. Penguin, 1967.

Timothy Leary, R. Metzner and R. Alpert, *The Psychedelic Experience*. University Books, New York, 1964.

George Birdwood, *The Willing Victim*. Secker and Warburg, 1969.

Kenneth Leech, *The Drug Subculture*. Church of England Council for Social Aid, Church House, Dean's Yard, London, SW1, 1968.

Kenneth Leech and Brenda Jordan, *Drugs For Young People: Their Use and Misuse*. Religious Education Press, Pergamon Press, 1967.

National Council for Civil Liberties, *Drugs and Civil Liberties*. From NCCL, 4 Camden High Street, London NW1.

Martin Silberman, *Aspects of Drug Addiction*. Royal London Prisoners Aid Society, 56 Stamford Street, London SE1, 1967.

Sally Trench, *Bury Me In My Boots*. Hodder, 1968.

C. W. Wilson and Arnold Linken (Ed.), *Adolescent Drug Dependence*. Pergamon, 1968.

G. E. W. Wolstenholme and Julie Knight, *Hashish: Its Chemistry and Pharmacology*. J. and A. Churchill, 1965.

Anthony J. Wood, *Drug Dependence*. Bristol Health Department, Tower Hill, Bristol 2. 1967.

Frank W. Wilson, *Microscope On Bondage*. Oliphants, 1968.

For a more comprehensive book list together with notes, write to Life for the World Publications, Northwick Park, Blockley, Moreton-in-Marsh, Glos. GL56 9RG.